SCIENCE
—AND—
RELIGION

IN SEARCH OF COSMIC PURPOSE

Edited by John F. Haught

GEORGETOWN UNIVERSITY PRESS
WASHINGTON, DC

SCIENCE
AND
RELIGION

IN SEARCH OF COSMIC PURPOSE

Edited by John F. Haught

CONTRIBUTORS

FRANCISCO J. AYALA	ANINDITA BALSLEV	OWEN GINGERICH
JOHN F. HAUGHT	ANDREI LINDE	SEYYED HOSSEIN NASR
BRIAN SWIMME	MARY EVELYN TUCKER

Georgetown University Press, Washington, D.C.
© 2000 by Georgetown University Press. All rights reserved.
Printed in the United States of America

10 9 8 7 6 5 4 3 2 1   2000

This volume is printed on acid-free offset book paper.

Library of Congress Cataloging-in-Publication Data

Science and religion in search of cosmic purpose / edited by John F.
    Haught.
        p.   cm.
    Includes bibliographical references and index.
    ISBN 0-87840-769-3 (cloth : alk. paper)
        1. Religion and science Congresses.   2. Teleology Congresses.
    I. Haught, John F.
    BL240.2.S276   2000
    291.1′75—dc21   99-36843
                                                            CIP

CONTENTS

Introduction   vii

1 | **Inflationary Cosmology and the Question of Teleology**   1
    Andrei Linde

2 | **Darwin and the Teleology of Nature**   18
    Francisco J. Ayala

3 | **Islamic Cosmology: Basic Tenets and Implications,**   42
    Yesterday and Today
    Seyyed Hossein Nasr

4 | **Cosmos and Consciousness: Indian Perspectives**   58
    Anindita Niyogi Balslev

5 | **Cosmology, Science, and Ethics in Japanese**   69
    Neo-Confucianism
    Mary Evelyn Tucker

6 | **Cosmic Directionality and the Wisdom of Science**   91
    Brian Swimme

7 | **Information and Cosmic Purpose**   105
    John F. Haught

8 | **Is There Design and Purpose in the Universe?**   121
    Owen Gingerich

Contributors:

Francisco J. Ayala is the Donald Bren Professor in the Department of Ecology and Evolutionary Biology at the University of California, Irvine. He is the author of over 600 articles and the book *Genetic Variation and Evolution,* coauthor of *Modern Genetics* (1984), and editor or coeditor of the following books: *Studies in the Philosophy of Biology* (1974), *Molecular Evolution* (1976), *Evolving: The Theory and Processes of Organic Evolution* (1979), *Population and Evolutionary Genetics: a Primer* (1982), and *Tempo and Mode in Evolution: Genetics and Paleontology 50 Years after Simpson* (1995). Ayala also served as the president and chairman of the board of the American Association for the Advancement of Science in 1994 and 1995.

Anindita Balslev is a professor in the Department of Philosophy at the University of Copenhagen. A native of India, Balslev received her doctorate in philosophy from the University of Paris. She is especially interested in the concepts of physical time and cosmic teleology. She is the author of *A Study of Time in Indian Philosophy* (1983), *Religious Tolerance or Acceptance* (1987), editor of *Cross-Cultural Conversation: Initiation* (1996), and coeditor of *Religion and Time* (1993).

Owen Gingerich is professor of astronomy and the history of science at Harvard University. His interests include creation and modern cosmogony and science and theology in the history of astronomy. In addition to numerous scientific articles, he has written or edited over twenty books, including *A Source Book in Astronomy and Astrophysics, 1900–1975* (editor, 1979), *Planetary, Lunar, and Solar Positions: New and Full Moons, A.D. 1650–1805* (coeditor, 1983), *The Eye of Heaven: Ptolemy, Copernicus, Kepler* (author, 1993), *The Nature of Scientific Discovery: A Symposium Commemorating the 500th Anniversary of the Birth of Nicholaus Copernicus* (editor, 1975), *The Wittich Connection: Conflict and Priority in Late Sixteenth-Century Cosmology* (coeditor, 1988), *The Physical Sciences in the Twentieth Century* (author, 1989), and *The Great Copernicus Chase and Other Adventures in Astronomical History* (author, 1992).

John F. Haught is professor of theology at Georgetown University, and director of the Georgetown Center for the Study of Science and Religion.

He is the author of ten books, including *The Cosmic Adventure: Science, Religion and the Quest for Purpose* (1984), *What Is God? How to Think about the Divine* (1986), *What Is Religion? An Introduction* (1990), *The Promise of Nature: Ecology and Cosmic Purpose* (1993), *Mystery and Promise: A Theology of Revelation* (1993), *Science and Religion: From Conflict to Conversation* (1995), and *God after Darwin: A Theology of Evolution* (1999).

Andrei Linde is professor of physics at Stanford University where, among other projects, he has developed the "inflationary" big bang theory. He studied at the Lebedev Physical Institute and Moscow State University in the former Soviet Union before coming to the United States. His research includes quantum cosmology, elementary particle physics, and the large-scale structure of the universe. Linde is widely considered to be one of the world's most distinguished cosmologists. He is the author of *Particle Physics and Inflationary Cosmology* (1990) and *Inflation and Quantum Cosmology* (1990), along with numerous scientific articles.

Seyyed Hossein Nasr, professor in the Department of Islamic Studies at George Washington University, is a leading philosopher and historian of science. He is author of numerous scholarly articles and books, including *Islam and the Plight of Modern Man* (1975), *Ideals and Realities of Islam* (1975), *An Introduction to Islamic Cosmological Doctrines* (1978), *Living Sufism* (1980), *Knowledge and the Sacred* (1981), *Islamic Life and Thought* (1981), *Islamic Art and Spirtuality* (1987), *Sufi Essays* (1991), *The Need for a Sacred Science* (1993), *Religion and the Order of Nature* (1996), and *Man and Nature: The Spiritual Crisis in Modern Man* (1997).

Brian Swimme is a mathematical cosmologist who teaches in the Department of Philosophy, Cosmology, and Consciousness at the California Institute for Integral Studies. In addition to numerous articles and book chapters, he is the author of *The New Natural Selection* (1983), *The Universe Is a Green Dragon* (1988), *The Hidden Heart of the Cosmos* (1996), and coauthor of *The Universe Story* (1994). Swimme has lectured broadly on the cultural, religious, and ecological implications of contemporary cosmology. He has also participated in BBC and PBS television programs on evolution and cosmology.

Mary Evelyn Tucker is a professor in the Department of Religion and the Program of East Asian Studies at Bucknell University. She is a leading expert on the history of Chinese and Japanese philosophies and cultures, especially Neo-Confucianism. Tucker is the author of *Moral and Spiritual Cultivation in Japanese Neo-Confucianism: The Life and Thought of Kaibara Ekken* (1989) and *Education and Ecology: Earth Literacy and the Technological Trance* (1993). Her interest in religions and ecology is evident in the books she has coedited: *Worldviews and Ecology: Religion, Philosophy, and the Environment* (1994), *Confucianism and Ecology: The Interrelation of Heaven, Earth, and Humans* (1998), and *Buddhism and Ecology: The Interconnection of Dharma and Deeds* (1999).

Introduction

Until the advent of modern science, human visions of reality were shaped by cultural and religious myths, most of which attributed an overarching "purpose" to the universe. In this age of science, however, many scientists and philosophers claim that our new knowledge offers little support for the existence of cosmic purpose or "teleology." Some even suggest that natural science confirms the pessimistic view that the universe is essentially "pointless" and hence indifferent to humanity's ageless quest for meaning.[1]

Not all scientists share this view, however, and some would even argue that contemporary scientific knowledge is remarkably consonant with a religious sense of purpose in the universe.[2] At the very least, scientists and scientific thinkers are now more willing than ever to converse with theologians and religious scholars on the question of whether the cosmic visions of the world's great spiritual traditions can be reclaimed in an age of science.

The conference "Cosmology and Teleology" that led to the essays presented here is an example of such a conversation. Cosponsored by the Georgetown Center for the Study of Science and Religion and the American Association for the Advancement of Science's Program on Dialogue between Science and Religion, the conference deliberately sought out prominent scholars representing a wide range of perspectives on both cosmology and religion. Our objective was to have them candidly address the question of cosmic purpose from within their diverse disciplinary fields or in the context of distinct cultural and religious traditions. Although several participants were understandably reluctant to address this difficult question head-on, they nonetheless provided perspectives that must be taken into account whenever we ask today whether scientific learning plausibly permits a retrieval of the substance of classic religious and philosophical teachings about cosmic meaning.

The symposium took place in Seattle, February 1997, in conjunction with the annual meeting of the American Association for the Advancement of Science. It began with Andrei Linde's summation of his innovative cosmological speculations about the possible existence of many "universes." A theoretician of the "inflationary" big bang theory, Linde is one of the world's most distinguished contemporary cosmologists. He received his training from the Lebedev Physical Institute and Moscow State University in the former Soviet Union, and when he immigrated to the United States nine years ago, he was appointed professor of physics at Stanford University. There he continues his research in quantum cosmology, elementary particle physics, and the large-scale structure of the universe.

In Chapter 1, Dr. Linde summarizes his highly original theory of a self-reproducing inflationary universe, one based on a nonlinear, fractal model of a multi-universe. His provocative version of inflationary cosmology would not require a cosmic "beginning," as do most interpretations of the standard big bang theory. While Linde would certainly agree that we do not as yet have any concrete evidence of the existence of the many "bubble universes" that his theory proposes, such a dizzying scenario as he pictures nonetheless raises important questions concerning what possible "meaning" contemporary theology and philosophy could associate with such a cosmos. Linde has given us a picture of things that leads us back to an appreciation of the enormity of mystery that enshrouds cosmic reality. The fathomless character of his multi-verse is a feature of no little significance at a time when other prominent physicists are dreaming of a final theory of nature that will allegedly dispel the domain of mystery from our consciousness once and for all.[3]

Our next contributor is Francisco Ayala, Donald Bren Professor in the Department of Ecology and Evolutionary Biology at the University of California, Irvine. Ayala is a native of Madrid, and an internationally recognized evolutionary biologist and population geneticist. Immigrating to the United States in 1961, he received his doctorate at Columbia University, where he studied with Theodosius Dobzhansky. He also served as the president and chairman of the board of the American Association for the Advancement of Science in 1994 and 1995. A prolific author (ten books and over 600 articles), and frequent lecturer abroad, he has strongly supported close collaboration between scientists and scholars in other disciplines, including theology.

Ayala's essay approvingly recites the standard neo-Darwinian understanding of evolution, according to which the blind, unguided, and "mechanical" process of natural selection provides, at least for science, the "ultimate explanation" of life and its diversity. His essay sharply raises the question as to whether there may be room alongside of science for a religiously teleological explanation of life. Ayala asserts his recurrent claim that Darwinian explanation *excludes* any appeal to the notion of God in accounting for the "design" in organisms. Biological science, he observes, has no difficulty acknowledging the teleological properties of organisms— the heart, for example, has the "purpose" of pumping blood. But the existence of such purposive features in living beings is not the product of divine design. Rather, it is the outcome of an utterly nonteleological process of natural selection that favors only those organisms that *happen* to be reproductively fit. After Darwin the ancient idea that nature is purposive in any overarching sense seems to Ayala to be completely unnecessary.

The mechanistic neo-Darwinian understanding of life expressed so clearly by Ayala would strike our next contributor as one of the most objectionable consequences of "modern" science's methodological exclusion of final causal considerations from its conception of nature. Representing an Islamic perspective on nature and purpose is Seyyed Hossein Nasr, now professor in the Department of Islamic Studies at George Washington University. Having received advanced training in physical sciences and philosophy at the Massachusetts Institute of Technology and Harvard University, Nasr has become a leading philosopher and historian of science. He is author of numerous books on Islamic science, philosophy, biography, art, and culture, and has published papers in Persian, Arabic, English, and French. He has also written a great deal on the question of cosmology and teleology in the light of modern science and what he considers to be its emaciated understanding of the natural world.

In Chapter 3 of this book Nasr compares the perspectives of modern science as it developed in the West since the sixteenth and seventeenth centuries with prominent cosmologies and scientific theories in the world of Islamic thought. He maintains that modernity's methodological exclusion of teleological considerations from our knowledge of nature, when combined with the very nonscientific claim that such knowledge is "ultimate," exhaustive, or adequate, has seriously impoverished our comprehension of the natural world. An advocate of what he calls a "sacred science," Nasr here summarizes some of the contributions Islamic thought can make toward what he takes to be a much more integral vision of nature than the one provided by modern science.

An Indian perspective on the question of science and cosmic purpose is offered by Anindita Balslev, professor in the Department of Philosophy at the University of Copenhagen. A native of India, Balslev received her graduate degrees from Calcutta University and a doctorate in philosophy from the University of Paris. She has published a number of important multidisciplinary studies of scientific theories, comparing different cultures and religious traditions. Her scholarly work has given special emphasis to the concepts of physical time and cosmic teleology.

Dr. Balslev's essay provides an examination of the perennial quest for the significance of human existence in the universe, especially as this is expressed in Eastern cultures. She argues forcefully that contemporary efforts to understand the universe can profit from the Indian emphasis on the inseparability of cosmos from consciousness. Unfortunately, as nature is interpreted in modern Western thought, it cannot be a repository of meaning, since the scientific mindset has already dualistically set the natural world apart from "consciousness," turning it into a sphere of aimless predictability. Given the modern conception of a cosmos divorced from consciousness, there can be no surprise that the universe will seem "pointless" to many scientists. Balslev, however, invites us to reexamine, in the light of Indian wisdom, what she takes to be the narrow and provincial modern assumption that the cosmos is essentially separable from consciousness.

Mary Evelyn Tucker, a professor in the Department of Religion and the East Asian Studies Program at Bucknell University, finds it fruitful for us to look at the cosmos afresh from the perspective of neo-Confucianism. Tucker is a leading expert on the history of Chinese and Japanese philosophies and cultures, especially neo-Confucianism. Her interests also include the relationship of ecology to the world's religious traditions, an area in which she has made numerous contributions.

Dr. Tucker's chapter in this book demonstrates that although Confucianism would not look for "cosmic purpose" in the manner of Western theism, it does not, for all that, view the universe as in any sense "pointless." By comparison with the modern sense of nature, the neo-Confucianist universe is "moral" and "meaningful"—indeed, a model for our own conduct as well as a place in which we humans can feel quite at home.

Brian Swimme's contribution to this volume seeks to bring together the traditional consensus that we live in a meaningful universe with what may be called a postmodern evolutionary vision of the cosmos. Swimme is a mathematical cosmologist who teaches in the Department of Philosophy, Cosmology, and Consciousness at the California Institute for Integral Studies. He lectures widely to academic audiences and the general public on physics, cosmology, philosophy, and ecology. He has also participated in the production of BBC and PBS television programs on evolutionary theories of the creation of the universe, ranging from the cosmic big bang to the emergence of life on earth.

Dr. Swimme argues that it is completely consistent with the most reliable scientific knowledge available today to speak of several kinds of "directionality" in the universe. A comparison of later with earlier phases of the fifteen-billion-year cosmic process will exhibit, for example, a general trend toward increasingly expansive differentiation, toward more complex instances of "autopoiesis" (creative self-organization), and toward increasingly complex interrelatedness of entities in the universe over the course of cosmic history since the big bang. The really interesting question, then, is not so much whether there is direction to the cosmic process—quite clearly there is—but how we humans should now understand our relationship to the universe from which we and other living beings have emerged. Refraining from any theological speculation on the remarkable cosmic trends he has highlighted, Swimme is content to make the point that our relatively new awareness of the world's ongoing evolution requires a revolution in our understanding of the place of human existence within an evolving universe. This in turn calls for a radical transformation of ethical life.

John F. Haught is professor of theology at Georgetown University and director of the Georgetown Center for the Study of Science and Religion. The essay included here argues that a biblically based notion of a purposeful cosmos is not at all incommensurate with the latest scientific understanding of nature. The notion of "information," which has gained considerable currency in contemporary science, allows us to hold simultaneously a belief in evolutionary science and a religious trust in cosmic meaning. Theology can coherently affirm the presence of divine action in the universe as well as a broad notion of cosmic purpose without in any way contradicting or intruding on the work of science itself.

The final contribution is by Owen Gingerich, professor of astronomy and the history of science at Harvard University. He has written on the censorship of Copernicus and on "The Galileo Affair." His interests include creation and modern cosmogony, theology and science, and science and theology in the history of astronomy. With this background he is uniquely poised to place in historical perspective recent controversial discussions by physicists concerning the so-called anthropic principle and its relationship to the question of teleology in nature. In the concluding chapter of this book, he takes up the question of whether astrophysics might point us in the direction of a restoration of natural theology, with its conviction that the universe is shaped by a transcendent, divine intelligence. In spite of the repudiation of cosmic purpose by leading evolutionists, Gingerich still wonders at the astonishing details of the natural order and at the fact that the big bang and stellar evolution exhibit a patterning in which "everything seems astonishingly well tuned for a universe in which self-conscious life can emerge."

******

The editor would like to express his deepest gratitude to Karim Ahmed for his tireless work and efficiency in organizing the conference "Cosmology and Teleology" on behalf of the Georgetown Center for the Study of Science and the American Association for the Advancement of Science (AAAS) Program on Dialogue between Science and Religion. Without his endless energy and expertise, the symposium could not have occurred. Special thanks are also extended to Audrey Chapman, director of the AAAS Program on Dialogue between Science and Religion, and her staff, for their co-sponsorship and support of this project.

This project was funded by grants from the John Templeton Foundation and the Esther A. and Joseph Klingenstein Fund, Inc. Their generosity has made possible both the conference "Cosmology and Teleology" and the present book.

Notes

1. For example, Steven Weinberg, *The First Three Minutes* (New York: Basic Books, 1997), p. 144.
2. See Ted Peters (ed.) *Science and Theology: The New Consonance* (New York: Westview Press, 1998).
3. See John Horgan, *The End of Science* (Reading, Massachusetts: Addison-Wesley Publishing Company, Inc., 1996).

1 | INFLATIONARY COSMOLOGY AND THE QUESTION OF TELEOLOGY

ANDREI LINDE

The Big Bang

According to the standard big bang theory, the universe was born at some moment ($t = 0$) about fifteen billion years ago, in a state of infinitely high temperature (T) and density (r) (cosmological singularity). The temperature of the expanding universe gradually decreased, allowing for its evolution into the relatively cold universe in which we live now. Remnants of the primordial cosmic fire still surround us in the form of microwave background radiation with a temperature of 2.7°K.

This theory has been extremely successful in explaining various features of our world. However, fifteen years ago physicists realized that it was plagued with many complicated problems. For example, standard big bang theory, when combined with the modern theory of elementary particles, predicts the existence of a large amount of superheavy stable particles carrying magnetic charge: magnetic monopoles. These objects have a typical mass 10^{16} times that of the proton. According to the standard big bang theory, monopoles should appear at the very early stages of the evolution of the universe, and they should now be as abundant as protons. In that case the mean density of matter in the universe would be about fifteen orders of magnitude higher than its present value of about 10^{-29} g/cm^3.

Originally there was some hope that this problem would disappear when more complicated theories of elementary particles were formulated. Unfortunately, despite the rapid development of elementary particle physics, the monopole problem remained unsolved, and many new ones have been added to the list. This forced physicists to look more attentively at the basic assumptions of the standard cosmological theory, and it appears that many of these assumptions are very suspicious.

The main problem with big bang cosmology is the very existence of the big bang. One may wonder what there was before the big bang. Where did the universe come from? If space-time did not exist for times less than 0, how could everything appear from nothing? What appeared first: the universe, or the laws determining its evolution? When we were born, the laws determining our development were written in the genetic code of our parents. But where were the laws of physics written when there was as yet no universe?

This problem of cosmological singularity still remains the most difficult problem of modern cosmology. However, as we shall see, we can now look at it from a totally different perspective. Let us now try to understand the question in much simpler terms. At school we were taught that two parallel lines never meet. According to the theory of general relativity, however, our universe is curved. The universe may be open, in which case the parallel lines diverge from one another; or it may be closed, with the parallel lines crossing each other like meridian lines on a globe. The only natural length parameter in general relativity is the Planck length $l_p \sim 10^{-33}$ cm. What this means is that one would expect our space to be very curved, with a typical radius of curvature about 10^{-33} cm. We can see, though, that our universe is just about flat on a scale of 10^{28} cm, the radius of the observable part of the universe. The results of our observations differ from our theoretical expectations by more than sixty orders of magnitude!

Let us ask another naive question: Why are there so many different people on the Earth? Of course, the Earth is large, so it can accommodate a lot of people. But why is the Earth so large? It is extremely small compared with the whole universe. But why, then, is the universe so large? Let us consider the universe of a typical size l_p with a Planck density, just emerging from the big bang. One can calculate how many particles such a universe would contain. The answer appears to be rather unexpected: the whole universe should contain just a few particles, not the 10^{88} particles contained in the part of the universe we see now. This is a contradiction by eighty-eight orders of magnitude.

The standard assumption of the big bang theory is that all parts of the universe began their expansion simultaneously at the moment $t = 0$. But how could different parts of the universe synchronize the beginning of their expansion if they did not have any time for it? Do we need to assume that there was some agent that initiated this process?

Our universe on the very large scale is extremely homogeneous. On the scale of 10^{10} light years the distribution of matter departs from perfect homogeneity by less than one part in a hundred thousand. For a long time nobody had any idea why the universe was so homogeneous. Those who do not have good ideas sometimes resort to principles. One of the cornerstones of the standard cosmology, for example, was the "cosmological principle," which asserts that the universe must be homogeneous. However, this does not help much, since the universe contains stars, galaxies, and other important deviations from homogeneity, so we have two opposite problems to solve. First, we must explain why our universe is so homogeneous, and second, we need to suggest what mechanism produced the galaxies and cosmic heterogeneity.

All of these problems (and others we have not mentioned) are extremely difficult. It is very encouraging, however, that most of these problems can be resolved in the context of one simple scenario of the evolution of the universe—the inflationary scenario.[1]

Particle Physics and Cosmology

To explain basic features of inflationary cosmology, we shall first make an excursion into the theory of elementary particles. The rapid progress of the inflationary theory during the last two decades became possible only after physicists found a way to unify weak, strong, and electromagnetic interactions.

It is well known that electrically charged particles interact with each other by creating an electromagnetic field around themselves. Small excitations of this field are called photons. Photons do not have any mass, which is the main reason why electrically charged particles can easily interact with each other at very large distances. Scientists believe that weak and strong interactions are mediated by similar particles. For example, weak interactions are mediated by particles called W and Z. However, whereas photons are massless particles, the particles W and Z are extremely heavy; it is very difficult to produce them. That is why weak interactions are so weak. To obtain a unified description of weak and electromagnetic interactions, despite the obvious difference in properties of photons and the W and Z particles, physicists introduced the notion of scalar fields f, which will play a central role in our discussion.

The theory of scalar fields is very simple. The closest analog of a scalar field is the electrostatic potential F. Electric and magnetic fields E and H appear only if this potential is nonhomogeneous or if it changes over time. If the whole universe would have the same electrostatic potential, say, 110 volts, then nobody would notice it; it would be just another vacuum state. Similarly, a constant scalar field f looks like a vacuum state; we do not see it even if we are surrounded by it.

The main point is that the constant electrostatic field F does not have its own energy, whereas the scalar field f may have potential energy density $V(f)$. If $V(f)$ has one minimum at $f = f_0$, then the whole universe eventually becomes filled by the field f_0. This field is invisible, but if it interacts with particles W and Z, they become heavy. Meanwhile, if photons do not interact with the scalar field, they remain light. Therefore, we may begin with a theory in which all particles initially are light and there is no fundamental difference between weak and electromagnetic interactions. This difference appears later, when the universe becomes filled by the scalar field f. At this moment the symmetry between different types of fundamental interactions is broken. This is the basic idea of all unified theories of weak, strong, and electromagnetic interactions.

Note that the existence of scalar fields makes its own contribution to the uniqueness problem: if the potential energy density $V(f)$ has more than one minimum, then the field f may occupy any of them. This means that the same theory may have different "vacuum states," corresponding to different types of symmetry-breaking between fundamental interactions, and, as a result, to different laws in the physics of elementary particles. To be more precise, one should speak about different laws of low-energy physics. At an extremely high energy, the difference in mass is not very important, and the initial symmetry of all fundamental interactions reveals itself again.

Finally, we should mention that in many theories of elementary particles popular today, it is assumed that space-time originally has considerably more than four dimensions. But these extra dimensions have been "compactified," shrunk to a very small size. That is why we cannot move in the corresponding directions, and our space-time looks four dimensional. However, one may wonder why compactification stopped with four effective space-time dimensions instead of two or five. Moreover, in the higher-dimensional theories compactification may occur in a thousand different ways. The values of coupling constants and particle masses after compactification strongly depend on the way compactification occurs. It becomes increasingly difficult to construct theories that admit only one type of compactification and only one way of symmetry-breaking.

This adds yet another problem to our list, which I call the "uniqueness problem." The essence of this problem was formulated by Albert Einstein: "What I am really interested in is whether God could have created the world differently." A few years ago it would have seemed rather meaningless to ask why our space-time is four dimensional, why the gravitational constant is so small, why the proton is 2,000 times heavier than the electron, etc. Now these questions have acquired a simple physical meaning and we cannot ignore them anymore. As we shall see, inflationary theory may help to answer these questions as well.

Inflationary Cosmology

According to the big bang theory, the rate of expansion of the universe given by the Hubble "constant" $H(t)$ is (approximately) proportional to the square root of its density. If the universe is filled with ordinary matter, then its density rapidly decreases as the universe expands. Therefore, the expansion of the universe rapidly slows down as its density decreases. This rapid decrease of the rate of the expansion of the universe is the main source of all our problems with the standard big bang theory. However, because of the equivalence of mass and energy established by Einstein ($E = mc^2$), the potential energy density $V(f)$ of the scalar field f also contributes to the rate of expansion of the universe. In certain cases the energy density $V(f)$ decreases much more slowly than the density of ordinary matter. This may lead to a stage of extremely rapid expansion (inflation) of the universe.

Let us consider the simplest model of a scalar field f with a mass m and with the potential energy density $V(\emptyset) = (m^2/2)\,\emptyset^2$. Since this function has a minimum at $f = 0$, one may expect that the scalar field f should oscillate near this minimum. This is indeed the case if the universe does not expand. However, one can show that in a rapidly expanding universe the scalar field moves down very slowly, as a ball in a viscous liquid, viscosity being proportional to the speed of expansion.

Now we have only one step further to go in order to understand where inflation comes from. If the scalar field f was initially large, its energy density $V(f)$ was also large, and the universe expanded very rapidly. Because of this rapid expansion f was moving to the minimum of $V(f)$ very slowly, as a ball in a viscous liquid. Therefore, at this stage the energy density $V(f)$, unlike the density of ordinary matter, remained almost constant, and expansion of the universe continued with a much greater speed than in the old cosmological theory: the size of the universe in this regime grows approximately as e^{Ht} where H is the Hubble "constant" proportional to the square root of $V(f)$.[2]

This stage of self-sustained exponentially rapid expansion of the universe was not very long. In a realistic version of our model its duration could be as short as 10^{-35} seconds. When the energy density of f becomes sufficiently small, viscosity also becomes small, inflation ends, and f

begins to oscillate near the minimum of $V(f)$. As with any rapidly oscillating classical field, it loses its energy by creating pairs of elementary particles. These particles interact with each other and come to a state of thermal equilibrium with some temperature T. From this time on, the corresponding part of the universe can be described by the standard hot universe theory.

The main difference between inflationary theory and the old cosmology becomes clear when one calculates the size of a typical inflationary domain at the end of inflation. Investigation of this question shows that even if the size of the part of the inflationary universe at the beginning of inflation in our model was as small as $lp \sim 10^{-33}$ cm, after 10^{-35} seconds of inflation this domain acquires the huge size of $l \sim 10^{10^{12}}$ cm! These numbers are model-dependent, but in all realistic models this size appears to be many orders of magnitude greater than the size of the part of the universe which we can see now, $l \sim 10^{28}$ cm. This immediately solves most of the problems associated with the old cosmological theory.

The question of why the universe is so homogeneous is solved, because all nonhomogeneities were stretched $10^{10^{12}}$ times. The density of primordial monopoles, domain walls, gravitinos, and other undesirable "defects" becomes exponentially diluted by inflation. (Recently we have found that in certain cases monopoles and domain walls inflate themselves and effectively push themselves out of the part of the universe that we can see.) The universe becomes enormously large. Even if it were a closed universe of a size $\sim 10^{-33}$ cm, after inflation the distance between its "South" and "North" poles becomes many orders of magnitude greater than 10^{28} cm. We see only a tiny part of the huge cosmic balloon. That is why the universe looks so flat, and why nobody has ever seen how parallel lines cross. It is also why we do not need the expansion of the universe to begin simultaneously in 10^{88} different causally disconnected domains of a Planck size. One such domain is enough to produce everything that we can see now!

Different Versions of Inflationary Theory

The idea that the universe at the first stages of its evolution should expand exponentially—being in an unstable vacuum state—was proposed in 1965 by Erast Gliner of the Institute of Physics and Technology, Leningrad.[3] This was the same year that Andrei Sakharov made a first attempt to calculate density perturbations generated by quantum fluctuations in this scenario. Afterwards, many other people speculated about this possibility. However, these speculations did not have sufficient scientific foundation, and until the primordial monopole problem was solved in 1978, nobody took these ideas seriously.

The first realistic version of inflationary theory was proposed in 1979 by Alexei Starobinsky of Landau Institute, Moscow.[4] Starobinsky's model created a sensation among Russian astrophysicists, and for two years it remained the main topic of discussion at all conferences on cosmology in the Soviet Union. This model, based as it was on the theory of anomalies in quantum gravity, was rather complicated.

A much simpler version was developed in 1981 by Alan Guth, now of MIT.[5] His model was based on the theory of cosmological phase transitions with supercooling, developed in the mid-1970s by David Kirzhnits and myself at the Lebedev Institute, Moscow.[6] Guth supposed that the universe originally was hot, but then at the epoch of the phase transitions it "supercooled"—remained trapped in a state where the forces were symmetric, even though that state had a greater energy than the state in which the symmetry among the forces was broken. Because it was trapped in that higher energy state, the universe had excess energy, and this forced it to expand very rapidly. This scenario was very attractive, and it had a very clear physical motivation. Unfortunately, as Guth himself has found, the universe after inflation in his scenario becomes extremely nonhomogeneous. After a year of investigation of his model, Guth finally rejected it in his paper with Eric Weinberg of Columbia University.[7]

In 1982 I introduced the so-called new inflationary universe scenario, which later was also developed by Andreas Albrecht and Paul Steinhardt at the University of Pennsylvania.[8] This scenario was free of the main problems of the model suggested by Guth: The phase transition from the high density vacuum state was very smooth, and the universe after inflation was rather homogeneous. Still, this model was complicated and somewhat artificial, and no realistic versions of this scenario have been proposed so far.

A year later, however, I realized that inflation can naturally occur in many theories of elementary particles, including the simplest theory of the scalar field discussed above. There is no need for quantum gravity effects, phase transitions, and supercooling. One should consider all possible chaotic distributions of the scalar field in the early universe, and then check whether some of them lead to inflation. Those places where inflation does not occur remain small, whereas those domains where inflation takes place become exponentially large and are the main contributors to the total volume of the universe. I called this scenario "chaotic inflation".[9] It is so simple that it is hard to understand why it was not discovered twenty years ago. I think that the reason is purely psychological: we were hypnotized by the glorious past of the big bang theory. We were assuming that the whole universe was created at the same moment, that initially it was hot, and that the scalar field from the very beginning was at the minimum of its potential energy density. Once we began relaxing our commitment to these assumptions, however, we found that inflation was not an exotic phenomenon invoked by theorists for solving their problems. It is a very general regime that occurs in a wide class of theories, including many models with polynomial and exponential potentials $V(f)$.

Solving many difficult cosmological problems simultaneously by a rapid stretching of the universe may seem too good to be true. Indeed, if all nonhomogeneities were stretched away, how would we account for the irregular distribution of galaxies? The answer is that while removing previously existing nonhomogeneities, inflation at the same time created new ones. The basic mechanism can be understood as follows: According to quantum field theory, empty space is not entirely empty. It is filled with quantum fluctuations of all types of physical fields. These fluctuations can be regarded as waves of physical fields with all possible wavelengths. If the values of these fields, averaged over some macroscopically large time, vanish, then the space filled with these fields seems to us empty and can be called a vacuum.

In the inflationary universe, however, the vacuum structure is more complicated. Those waves that have a very short wavelength "do not know" that the universe is curved; they move in all directions with a speed approaching that of light. Inflation, however, very rapidly stretches these waves. Once their wavelengths become sufficiently large, these waves begin "feeling" that the universe is curved. At this moment they stop moving because of the effective viscosity of the expanding universe with respect to the scalar field.

The first quantum fluctuations to freeze are those with large wavelengths. The amplitude of the frozen waves does not change later, but their wavelengths grow exponentially. In the course of the expansion of the universe, new and then even newer fluctuations become stretched and freeze on top of each other. At that stage one can no longer call these waves "quantum fluctuations." Most of them have exponentially large wavelengths. These waves do not move and do not disappear, being averaged over large periods of time. What we get, then, is a nonhomogeneous distribution of the classical scalar field f that does not oscillate. It is this nonhomogeneity that is responsible for perturbations of density in our universe and for the subsequent appearance of galaxies.[10]

Self-Reproducing Universe

As we have already mentioned, one can visualize quantum fluctuations of the scalar field in the inflationary universe as waves that first move in all possible directions and then freeze on top of each other. Each freezing wave slightly increase the value of the scalar field in some parts of the universe, and slightly decreases this value in other parts of the universe.

Now let us consider those rare parts of the universe where these freezing waves always increase the value of the scalar field f, persistently pushing the scalar field uphill to the greater values of its potential energy $V(f)$. This is a very strange and obviously improbable regime. Indeed, the probability that the field f will make one jump up (instead of jump down), is equal to 1/2; the probability that the next time it also jumps up is also 1/2, so that the probability that the field f without any special reason will make N consecutive jumps in the same direction is extremely small; it will be proportional to $1/2^N$.

Normally, one neglects such fluctuations. However, in our case they can be extremely important. Indeed, those rare domains of the universe where the field jumps high enough begin expanding with exponentially increasing speed. Remember that an inflationary universe expands as e^{Ht}, where the Hubble constant is proportional to the square root of the energy density of the field f. In our simple model with $V(f) \sim \emptyset^2$, the Hubble constant H will be simply proportional to f. Thus, the higher the field f jumps, the faster the universe expands. Very soon those rare domains, where the field f persistently climbs up the wall, will acquire a much greater volume than those domains that keep sliding to the minimum of $V(f)$ in accordance with the laws of classical physics.

From our theory it follows that if the universe contains at least one inflationary domain of a sufficiently large size, it begins unceasingly to produce more and more new inflationary domains. Inflation at each particular point may end very quickly, but there will be many other places that will continue expanding exponentially. The total volume of all inflationary domains will grow without end. I call this process "eternal inflation."[11] In this scenario, the universe as a whole is immortal. Each particular part of the universe may appear from a singularity somewhere in the past, and it may end up in a singularity somewhere in the future. However, there is no end for the evolution of the whole universe.

The situation with regard to the beginning is less certain. It is most probable that each part of the inflationary universe has originated from some singularity in the past. However, at present we have no proof that all parts of the universe were created simultaneously in a general cosmological singularity before which there was no space and time at all. Moreover, the total number of inflationary bubbles on our "cosmic tree" grows exponentially over time. Therefore, most of the bubbles (including our own part of the universe) grow indefinitely far away from the root of this tree. This scenario removes the possible beginning of the whole universe to the indefinite past.

Until now we had considered the simplest inflationary model with only one scalar field f. In realistic models of elementary particles, however, there are many different scalar fields. For example, in the unified theories of weak and electromagnetic interactions there exist at least two other scalar fields, Φ and H. In some versions of these theories the potential energy density of the fields has about a dozen different minima of the same depth. During inflation these fields, just as the field f, jump in all possible directions due to quantum fluctuations. Then after inflation, they fall down to different minima of their energy density in different exponentially large parts of the universe. We should remember that scalar fields change properties of elementary particles and the laws of their interaction. This means that after inflation, the universe becomes divided into exponentially large domains possessing different laws of low-energy physics. It does not mean that the fundamental law governing our universe is not unique. The situation here can be understood if one thinks about different states of water: it can be in a solid, liquid, or gaseous state. It is the same water, but the states look quite different from each other, and fish can live only in the liquid form.

Note that if fluctuations are not too strong, scalar fields cannot jump from one minimum of their energy density to another. In this case the new parts of an inflationary universe would remember the "genetic code" of their parents. However, if fluctuations are sufficiently large, mutations will occur, and the "laws of physics" in new bubbles will vary from one bubble to another. In some inflationary models, quantum fluctuations become so strong that even the effective number of dimensions of space and time change. According to these models, we find ourselves inside a four-dimensional domain with our kind of physical laws not because domains with different dimensionality and with different particle properties are impossible or improbable, but simply because our kind of life cannot exist in other domains.

Cosmology and Teleology

Here, then, we arrive at a point where recent scientific discoveries may have implications for religious speculation about the origin and the fate of the universe. Indeed, they may seriously challenge some of our established religious beliefs. With the development of science it has become more and more difficult to talk about God in simplistic terms. Apparently, the laws of the universe work so precisely that we do not need the hypothesis of divine intervention in order to describe the behavior of the universe as we know it.

In the past there was one aspect of the universe hidden from us, apparently beyond explanation: the moment of creation of the universe as a whole. The mystery of creation of everything from nothing may have seemed too great to be considered scientifically. With the development of inflationary cosmology, however, the status of this mystery seems to have changed. The possibility that the universe eternally re-creates itself in all its various forms does not necessarily resolve the problem of creation, but it does push it back to the indefinite past.[12] As a result, the properties of our world become totally disentangled from the properties of the universe at the time of origin (if there was such a time at all). In other words, one may argue that the properties of our world do not represent the original design and cannot carry any message from a Creator whatsoever.

Is it true? Is this the final word of science? Instead of giving a definite answer to this question I would like to consider two radically different possibilities and invite the reader to think about them.

Creation of the Universe in a Laboratory
Recently there was a discussion of whether it is possible to create a universe in a laboratory. Indeed, one may need to have only a milligram of matter in a vacuum-like exponentially expanding state to allow the process of self-reproduction to create from this matter not one universe but infinitely many!

It is still not clear whether this process is theoretically possible or technologically feasible, but let us imagine that the answer to both of these questions is affirmative. Should we really try to build a new universe in a laboratory? How would one be able to use it? Of course, one could just consider the issue of the universe's creation as an interesting theoretical problem to think about in one's spare time, but if the universe's creation is entirely useless, one could presumably find more interesting problems to work on.

In any case, one cannot simply "pump" energy from the new universe to our own, since this would contradict the energy conservation law. And one cannot "jump" into the new universe, since at the moment of its creation it would be microscopically small and extremely dense, and later it would decouple from our universe. One cannot even send any information about oneself to any conscious inhabitants of the new universe. If one tries, so to speak, to write something "on the surface of the universe," then, for billions of years to come, the inhabitants of the new universe will live in a corner of one letter. This is the consequence of a general rule: all local properties of the universe after inflation do not depend on initial conditions at the moment of its formation. Very soon the universe becomes absolutely flat, homogeneous, and isotropic, and any original message "imprinted" on it becomes unreadable.

We were able to find only one exception to this rule. As we already mentioned, if chaotic inflation starts at a sufficiently large energy density, then it goes on forever, creating more and more inflationary domains. These domains contain matter in all possible "phase states" (or vacuum states), corresponding to all possible minima of the effective potential and all possible types of laws of physics compatible with inflation. However, if inflation starts at a sufficiently low energy density, as is often the case with the universes produced in a laboratory, then no such diversification occurs; inflation at a relatively small energy density does not change the symmetry-breaking pattern of the theory and the way of compactification of space-time. Therefore, it seems that the only way to send a message to those who might live in the universe we are planning to create is to encrypt it into the properties of the vacuum state of the new universe, i.e., to the laws of low-energy physics. Hopefully, one may achieve this by choosing a proper combination of temperature, pressure, and external fields, which would lead to creation of the universe in a desirable phase state.

The corresponding message would be long and informative enough only if there are extremely many ways of symmetry-breaking and/or patterns of compactification in the underlying theory. This is exactly the case, for example, in the superstring theory, a feature that was considered for a long time to be one of the main problems resident in this theory. Another requirement for the informative message would be that it must not be too simple. If, for example, masses of all particles would be equal to each other, all coupling constants would be given by 1, etc., and the corresponding message would be too short. Perhaps one may communicate quite a lot of information by creating a universe in a strange vacuum state with the proton being 2,000 times heavier than the electron, W bosons being 100 times heavier than the proton, etc., i.e., in the vacuum state in which we live now. The stronger the symmetry-breaking and the more "unnatural" the relations between parameters of the theory after it, the more information the message may contain. Is this the reason why relations between particle masses and coupling constants in our universe look so bizarre? Does this mean that our universe was created by a hacker physicist?!

The possibility described above represents an ultimate example of the arrogance of science. One cannot simply ignore this possibility without a detailed investigation, but let us consider a possibility that points in an opposite direction.

Physics and Consciousness

If quantum mechanics is true, then one may try to find the wave function of the universe. This would allow us to find out which events are probable and which are not. However, this often leads to problems of interpretation. For example, at the classical level one can speak of the age of the universe t. However, the essence of the Wheeler-DeWitt equation, which is the Schrödinger equation for the wave function of the universe, is that this wave function *does not depend on time,* since the total Hamiltonian of the universe, including the Hamiltonian of the gravitational field, vanishes identically.[13] Therefore, if one wished to describe the evolution of the universe with the help of its wave function, one would be in trouble.

The resolution of this paradox is rather instructive. The notion of evolution is not applicable to the universe as a whole since there is no external observer with respect to the universe, and there is no external clock as well that would not belong to the universe. However, we do not actually ask why the universe as a whole is evolving in the way we see it. We are just trying to understand our own experimental data. Thus, a more precisely formulated question is why we see the universe evolving in time in a given way.

To answer this question one should first divide the universe into two main pieces: (a) an observer with his or her clock and other measuring devices, and (b) the rest of the universe. Then it can be shown that the wave function of the rest of the universe does depend on the state of the clock of the observer, i.e., on his or her "time." This time dependence in some sense is "objective," which means that the results obtained by different (macroscopic) observers living in the same quantum state of the universe and using sufficiently good (macroscopic) measuring apparatus agree with each other.

Thus, we see that by an investigation of the wave function of the universe as a whole one sometimes gets information that has no direct relevance to the observational data, e.g., that the universe does not evolve in time. To describe the universe *as we see it,* one should divide it into several macroscopic pieces and calculate a conditional probability to observe it in a given state under the obvious condition that the observer and his or her measuring apparatus do exist. Without introducing an observer, we have a dead universe, one that does not evolve in time.

This example demonstrates an unusually important role played by the concept of an observer in quantum cosmology. Most of the time, when discussing quantum cosmology, one can remain entirely within the bounds set by purely physical categories, regarding the observer simply as an automaton, and not dealing with questions of whether the observer has consciousness or feels anything during the process of observation. This we have done in all of the preceding discussions. But we cannot rule out *a priori* the possibility that carefully avoiding the concept of consciousness in quantum cosmology constitutes an artificial narrowing of one's outlook. A number of authors have underscored the complexity of the situation, replacing the word "observer" with the word "participant," and introducing such terms as "self-observing universe." In fact, the question may come down to whether standard physical theory is actually a closed system with regard to its description of the universe as a whole at the quantum level: Is it really possible to understand fully what the universe is without first understanding what life is?

Let us recall here an example from the history of science that may prove to be rather instructive. Prior to the advent of the special theory of relativity, space, time, and matter seemed to be three fundamentally different entities. In fact, space was thought to be a kind of three-dimensional coordinate grid which, when supplemented by clocks, could be used to describe the motion of matter. Special relativity, however, did away with the insuperable distinction between space and time, combining them into a unified whole. But space-time nevertheless remained something of a fixed arena in which the properties of matter became manifest. As before, space itself possessed no intrinsic degrees of freedom, and it continued to play a secondary, subservient role as a backdrop for the description of the truly substantial material world.

The general theory of relativity brought with it a decisive change in this point of view. Space-time and matter were found to be interdependent, and there was no longer any question of which was the more fundamental of the two. Space-time was also found to have its own inherent degrees of freedom, associated with perturbations of the metric gravitational waves. Thus, space can exist and change with time in the absence of electrons, protons, photons, etc.; in other words, in the absence of anything that had *previously* (i.e., prior to general relativity) been subsumed by the term "matter." (Note that because of the weakness with which they interact, gravitational waves are exceedingly difficult to detect experimentally— an as-yet unsolved problem.)

A more recent trend, finally, has been toward a unified geometric theory of all fundamental interactions, including gravitation. Prior to the end of the 1970s, such a program seemed unrealizable; rigorous theorems were proven on the impossibility of unifying spatial symmetries with the internal symmetries of elementary particle theory. Fortunately, these theorems were sidestepped after the discovery of supersymmetric theories. In principle, with the help of super-gravity, Kaluza-Klein, and superstring theories, one may hope to construct a theory in which all matter fields will be interpreted in terms of the geometric properties of some multidimensional superspace. Space would then cease to be simply a requisite mathematical adjunct for the description of the real world, and would instead take on greater and greater independent significance, gradually encompassing all the material particles under the guise of its own intrinsic degrees of freedom.

According to standard materialistic doctrine, consciousness, like space-time before the invention of general relativity, plays a secondary, subservient role, being considered just a function of matter and a tool for the description of the truly existing material world. It is certainly possible that nothing similar to the modification and generalization of the concept of space-time will occur with the concept of consciousness in the coming decades. However, I would like to take a risk here and formulate several questions to which we do not yet have the answers.

Is it not possible that consciousness, like space-time, has its own intrinsic degrees of freedom, and that neglecting these will lead to a description of the universe that is fundamentally incomplete? Might it not turn out, with the further development of science, that the study of the universe and the study of consciousness will be inseparably linked, and that ultimate progress in the one will be impossible without progress in the other? After the development of a unified geometrical description of the weak, strong, electromagnetic, and gravitational interactions, will the next important step not be the development of a unified approach to our entire world, including the world of consciousness?

All of these questions might seem somewhat naive, but to work in the field of quantum cosmology without an answer to them, and without even trying to discuss them, gradually becomes as difficult as working on the hot universe theory without knowing why there are so many different things in the universe, why nobody has ever seen parallel lines intersect, why the universe is almost homogeneous and looks approximately the same at different locations, why space-time is four-dimensional, and so on. Now that we have plausible answers to these questions, one can only be surprised that prior to the 1980s, it was sometimes taken to be bad form even to discuss them. The reason is really very simple: By asking such questions, one confesses one's own ignorance of the simplest facts of daily life, and moreover encroaches upon a realm that may seem not to belong to the world of positive knowledge. It is much easier to convince oneself that such questions do not exist, that they are somehow not legitimate, or that someone answered them long ago.

It would probably be best then not to repeat the old mistakes, but instead to acknowledge that the problem of consciousness and the related problem of human life and death are not only unsolved, but at a fundamental level are completely unexamined. It is tempting to seek connections and analogies of some kind, even if they are shallow and superficial ones at first, by studying one more great problem: that of the birth, life, and death of the universe. It may conceivably become clear at some future time that these two problems are not so disparate as they might seem.

Notes

1. A. D. Linde, *Particle Physics and Inflationary Cosmology* (Chur, Switzerland: Harwood, 1990), and *Inflation and Quantum Cosmology* (Boston: Academic Press, 1990).

2. To understand the situation at a more formal level, one should analyze two equations that describe inflation in our model: $\ddot{\o} + 3H\dot{\o} = -dV(\o)/d\o$, and $H^2 = 8\pi G/3\ V(\o)$. The second equation is a slightly simplified Einstein equation for the scale factor (radius) of the universe $a(t)$. H is a Hubble constant, $H = \dot{a}/a$, and G is the gravitational constant. The term $3H\dot{\phi}$ in the first equation is similar to the friction (viscosity) term in the equation of motion for a harmonic oscillator. One can show that if $V(f)$ is approximately constant during a sufficiently long period of time, the last equation has an inflationary solution $a(t) \sim e^{Ht}$.

3. E. B. Gliner, "Algebraic Properties of the Energy-momentum Tensor and Vacuum-like States of Matter," *Journal of Experimental and Theoretical Physics (USSR)*, 22 (1965), 378; *Doklady Akademia Naukma (USSR)* 192 (1970), 771; E. B. Gliner and I. G. Dymnikova, *Pisma Astronomical Zhournal (USSR)*, 1 (1975), 7; I. E. Gurevich, *Astrophysics Space Science*, 38 (1975), 67.

4. A. A. Starobinsky, "Spectrum of Relict Gravitational Radiation and the Early State of the Universe," *Journal of Experimental and Theoretical Physics, Letters (USSR)*, 30 (1979), 682; A. A. Starobinsky "A New Type of Isotropic Cosmological Models without Singularity," *Physics Letters* 91B (1980): 99.

5. A. H. Guth, "Inflationary Universe: A Possible Solution to the Horizon Flatness Problems," *Physical Review*, D23 (1981), 347.

6. D. A. Kirzhnits, "Weinberg Model and the 'Hot' Universe," *Journal of Experimental and Theoretical Physics Letters (USSR)*, 15 (1972), 529; D. A. Kirzhnits and A. D. Linde, "Macroscopic Consequences of the Weinberg Model," *Physics Letters*, 42B (1972), 471; "A Relativistic Phase Transition," *Journal of Experimental and Theoretical Physics (USSR)*, 40 (1974), 628; "Symmetry Behavior in Gauge Theories," *Annals of Physics*, 101 (1976), 195; S. Weinberg, *Physical Review*, D9 (1974), 3320; L. Dolan and R. Jackiw, "Symmetry Behavior at Finite Temperature," *Physical Review*, D9 (1974), 3357.

7. A. H. Guth and E. Weinberg, "Could the Universe Have Recovered from a Slow First-order Phase Transition?" *Nuclear Physics*, B212 (1983), 321.

8. A. D. Linde, "A New Inflationary Universe Scenario: a Possible Solution of the Horizon, Flatness, Homogeneity, Isotropy and Primordial Monopole Problems," *Physical Review Letters*, 108B (1982), 389; A. Albrecht and P. J. Steinhardt, "Cosmology for Grand Unified Theories with Radiatively Induced Symmetry Breaking," *Physical Review Letters*, 48 (1982), 1220.

9. A. D. Linde, "Chaotic Inflation," *Physical Review Letters*, 129B (1983), 177.

10. V. F. Mukhanov and G. V. Chibisov, "Quantum Fluctuations and a Nonsingular Universe," *Journal of Experimental and Theoretical Physics Letters (USSR)*, 33 (1981), 532; S. W. Hawking, "The Development of Irregularities in a Single Bubble Inflationary Universe," *Physical Review Letters*, 115B (1982), 295; A. A. Starobinsky, "Dynamics of Phase Transition in the New Inflationary Universe Scenario and Generation of Perturbations," *Physics Letters*, 117B (1982), 175; A. H. Guth and S.-Y. Pi, "Fluctuations in the New Inflationary Universe," *Physical Review Letters*, 49 (1982), 1110; J. Bardeen, P. J. Steinhardt, and M. Turner, "Spontaneous Creation of Almost Scale-free Density Perturbations in an Inflationary Universe," *Physical Review*, D28 (1983), 679.

11. A. D. Linde, "Externally Existing Self-reproducing Chaotic Inflationary Universe," *Physics Letters*, 175B (1986), 395; "Particle Physics and Inflationary Cosmology," *Physics Today*, 40 (1987), 61; "The Self-Reproducing Inflationary Universe," *Scientific American*, 271 (1994), 48; also in B. Zuckerman and M. A. Malkan, eds., *The Origin and Evolution of the Universe* (Sudbury, MA: Jones and Bartlett, 1996).

12. A. D. Linde, D. A. Linde, and A. Mezhlumian, "From the Big Bang Theory to the Theory of a Stationary Universe," *Physical Review*, D49 (1994), 1783.

13. The "Hamiltonian" is a mathematical function expressing the connection between energy and rates of change in a dynamic physical system.

2 | DARWIN AND THE TELEOLOGY OF NATURE

FRANCISCO J. AYALA

In this essay I argue that teleological explanations are necessary in order to give a full account of the attributes of living organisms, whereas they are neither necessary nor appropriate in the explanation of inanimate phenomena. I give a definition of teleology and clarify the matter by distinguishing between internal and external teleology, and between bounded and unbounded teleology. The human eye, so obviously constituted for seeing, but resulting from a natural process, is an example of internal (or natural) teleology. A knife has external (or artificial) teleology, because it has been purposefully designed by an external agent. The development of an egg into a chicken is an example of bounded (or necessary) teleology because it always develops into a chicken, whereas the evolutionary origin of the mammals is a case of unbounded (or contingent) teleology, because there was nothing in the make up of the first living cells that necessitated the eventual appearance of mammals.

The presence of teleology in living organisms is a distinctive consequence of the interactions of natural selection with mutation and other stochastic phenomena in the process of the adaptation of organisms to their environments. The outcome of this process is evolution, which is a creative process that can account for the appearance of genuine novelty. How natural selection "creates" is shown with a simple example and clarified with two analogies, artistic creation and the "typing monkeys," with which it shares important similarities and differences. The creative power of natural selection arises precisely from an interaction between chance and necessity, or between random and deterministic processes.

18

Darwin's Revolution

The concept of teleology is in general disrepute in modern science. More often than not it is considered to be a mark of superstition, or at least a vestige of the nonempirical, a prioristic approach to natural phenomena characteristic of the prescientific era. The main reason for this discredit is that the notion of teleology is equated with the belief that future events— the goals or end-products of processes—are active agents in their own realization. In evolutionary biology, teleological explanations are understood to imply the belief that there is a planning agent external to the world, or a force immanent in living beings, directing the evolutionary process toward the production of specified kinds of organisms. The nature and diversity of organisms are, then, explained teleologically in such a view as the goals or ends-in-view intended from the beginning by the Creator, or as a necessary development of specific potentialities implicit in the nature of the first organisms.

Biological evolution can, however, be explained without recourse to a Creator or a planning agent external to the organisms themselves. There is no evidence either of any vital force or immanent energy directing the evolutionary process toward the production of specified kinds of organisms. The evidence of the fossil record is against any directing force, external or immanent, leading the evolutionary process toward specified goals. Teleology understood in the stated sense is, then, appropriately rejected in biology as a category of explanation.

In *On the Origin of Species* Darwin accumulated an impressive number of observations supporting the evolutionary origin of living organisms. Moreover, and most important, he provided a causal explanation of evolutionary processes—the theory of natural selection. The principle of natural selection makes it possible to give a natural explanation of the adaptation of organisms to their environments. Darwin recognized, and accepted without reservation, that organisms are adapted to their environments, and that their parts are adapted to the functions they serve. Penguins are adapted to live in the cold, the wings of birds are made to fly, and the eye is made to see. Darwin accepted the facts of adaptation and then provided a natural explanation for the facts. One of his greatest accomplishments was to bring the teleological aspects of nature into the realm of science. He substituted a scientific teleology for a theological one. The teleology of nature could now be explained, at least in principle, as the result of natural laws manifested in natural processes, without recourse to an external Creator or to spiritual or nonmaterial forces. At that point biology came into maturity as a science.

The discoveries of Copernicus, Kepler, Galileo, and Newton in the sixteenth and seventeenth centuries had gradually ushered in a conception of the universe as consisting of matter in motion, governed by natural laws. It was shown that the earth is not the center of the universe, but a small planet rotating around an average star; that the universe is immense in space and in time; and that the motions of the planets around the sun can be explained by the same simple laws that account for the motion of physical objects on our planet. These and other discoveries greatly expanded human knowledge, but the conceptual revolution they brought about was even more fundamental: a commitment to the postulate that the universe obeys immanent laws that account for natural phenomena. The workings of the universe were thus brought into the realm of science, i.e., were explained through natural laws. Darwin completed the Copernican revolution by drawing out for biology the ultimate conclusion of the notion of nature as a lawful system of matter in motion. The adaptations and diversity of organisms, the origin of novel and highly organized forms, even the origin of mankind itself could now be explained by an orderly process of change governed by natural laws.

Before Darwin, the origin of organisms and their marvelous adaptations were left unexplained or were attributed to the design of an omniscient Creator. In the thirteenth century St. Thomas Aquinas had used the design of nature as his "fifth way" to demonstrate the existence of God. In the nineteenth century the English theologian William Paley, in *Natural Theology* (1802), elaborated the argument from design as a forceful demonstration of the existence of the Creator.[1] The functional design of the human eye, argued Paley, provided conclusive evidence of an all-wise Creator. It would be absurd to suppose, he wrote, that the human eye by mere chance "should have consisted, first, of a series of transparent lenses . . . secondly of a black cloth or canvas spread out behind these lenses so as to receive the image formed by pencils of light transmitted through them, and placed at the precise geometrical distance at which, and at which alone, a distinct image could be formed . . . thirdly of a large nerve communicating between this membrane and the brain." *The Bridgewater Treatises,* published between 1833 and 1840, were written by eminent scientists and philosophers to set forth "the Power, Wisdom, and Goodness of God as manifested in the Creation." The structure and mechanisms of the hand were, for example, cited as incontrovertible evidence that the hand had been designed by the same omniscient Power that had created the world.

The advances of physical science had thus driven mankind's conception of the universe to a schizophrenic state of affairs, which persisted well into the mid-nineteenth century. Scientific explanations, derived from natural laws, dominated the world of nonliving matter, on earth as well as in the heavens. Supernatural explanations, depending on the unfathomable deeds of the Creator, accounted for the origin and configuration of living creatures—the most diversified, complex, and interesting realities of the world. It was Darwin's genius to resolve this conceptual schizophrenia.

The strength of the argument from design is easily set forth. Wherever there is function or design we look for its author. A knife is made for cutting and a clock is made to tell time; their functional designs have been contrived by a knife-maker and a watchmaker. The exquisite design of Leonardo da Vinci's *Mona Lisa* proclaims that it was created by a gifted artist following a preconceived purpose. Similarly, the structures, organs, and behaviors of living beings are directly organized to serve certain functions. The functional design of organisms and their features would therefore seem to argue for the existence of a designer. It was Darwin's greatest accomplishment to show that the directive organization of living beings can be explained as the result of a natural process, natural selection, without any need to resort to a Creator or other external agent. The origin and adaptation of organisms in their profusion and wondrous variations were thus brought into the realm of science.

Darwin's theory encountered opposition in religious circles, not so much because he proposed the evolutionary origin of living things (which had been proposed before, and accepted even by Christian theologians), but because the causal mechanism, natural selection, excluded God as the explanation for the obvious design of organisms. The configuration of the universe was no longer the result of God's Design, but simply the outcome of immanent, blind processes.

Natural Selection, Design, and Novelty

The central argument of the theory of natural selection is summarized by Darwin in *The Origin of Species* as follows:

> As more individuals are produced than can possibly survive, there must in every case be a struggle for existence, either one individual with another of the same species, or with the individuals of distinct species, or with the physical conditions of life. ... Can it, then, be thought improbable, seeing that variations useful to man have undoubtedly occurred, that other variations useful in some way to each being in the great and complex battle of life, should sometimes occur in the course of

thousands of generations? If such do occur, can we doubt (remembering that more individuals are born than can possibly survive) that individuals having any advantage, however slight, over others, would have the best chance of surviving and of procreating their kind? On the other hand, we may feel sure that any variation in the least degree injurious would be rigidly destroyed. This preservation of favorable variation and the rejection of injurious variations, I call Natural Selection.[2]

Darwin's argument addresses the problem of explaining the adaptive character of organisms. Darwin argues that adaptive variations ("variations useful in some way to each being") occasionally appear, and that these are likely to increase the reproductive chances of their carriers. Over the generations, favorable variations will be preserved, injurious ones will be eliminated. In one place Darwin adds: "I can see no limit to this power [natural selection] in slowly and beautifully *adapting* each form to the most complex relations of life" (emphasis added). Natural selection was proposed by Darwin primarily to account for the adaptive organization, or "design," of living beings; it is a process that promotes or maintains adaptation. Evolutionary change through time, and evolutionary diversification (multiplication of species) are not directly promoted by natural selection (hence, the so-called evolutionary stasis of the theory of punctuated equilibrium), but they often ensue as by-products of natural selection fostering adaptation.

Darwin understood natural selection primarily as differential survival. The modern understanding of the principle of natural selection, on the other hand, is formulated in genetic and statistical terms as differential *reproduction*. Natural selection implies that some genes and genetic combinations are transmitted to the following generations on the average more frequently than their alternates. Such genetic units will become more common in every subsequent generation and their alternates less common. Natural selection, then, is a statistical bias in the relative rate of reproduction of alternative genetic units.

Natural selection has been compared with a sieve that retains the rarely arising useful genes and lets go of the more frequently arising harmful mutants. Natural selection acts in that way, but it is much more than a purely negative process, for it is able to generate novelty by increasing the probability of otherwise extremely improbable genetic combinations. Natural selection is thus creative, in a way. It does not "create" the entities upon which it operates, but it produces adaptive genetic combinations that would not have existed otherwise.

The creative role of natural selection must not be understood in the sense of the "absolute" creation that traditional Christian theology predicates of the divine act by which the universe was brought into being *ex nihilo*. Natural selection may rather be compared with a painter who creates a picture by mixing and distributing pigments in various ways over the canvas. The canvas and the pigments are not created by the artist, but the painting is. It is conceivable that a random combination of the pigments might result in the orderly whole, which is the final work of art. But the probability of Leonardo's *Mona Lisa* resulting from a random combination of pigments, or of St. Peter's Basilica resulting from a random association of marble, bricks, and other materials, is infinitely small. In the same way, the combination of genetic units that carries the hereditary information responsible for the formation of the vertebrate eye could never have been produced by a random process like mutation—not even if we allow for the more than three billion years during which life has existed on earth. The complicated anatomy of the eye, like the exact functioning of the kidney, is the result of a nonrandom process—natural selection.

How natural selection, a purely material process, can generate novelty in the form of accumulated hereditary information can be illustrated by the following example. Some strains of the colon bacterium *Escherichia coli,* in order to be able to reproduce in a culture medium, require that a certain substance, the amino acid histidine, be present in the medium. When a few such bacteria are added to a cubic centimeter of liquid culture medium, they multiply rapidly and produce between two and three billion bacteria in a few hours. Spontaneous mutations to streptomycin resistance occur in normal (i.e., sensitive) bacteria at rates on the order of one in one hundred million (1×10^{-8}) cells. In our bacterial culture we expect between twenty and thirty bacteria to be resistant to streptomycin due to spontaneous mutation. If a proper concentration of the antibiotic is added to the culture, only the resistant cells survive. The twenty or thirty surviving bacteria will start reproducing, however, and allowing a few hours for the necessary number of cell divisions, several billion bacteria are produced, all resistant to streptomycin. Among cells requiring histidine as a growth factor, spontaneous mutants able to reproduce in the absence of histidine arise at rates of about four in one hundred million (4×10^{-8}) bacteria. The streptomycin-resistant cells may now be transferred to a culture with streptomycin, but with no histidine. Most of them will not be able to reproduce, but about a hundred will start reproducing until the available medium is saturated.

Natural selection has produced in two steps bacterial cells resistant to streptomycin and not requiring histidine for growth. The probability of the two mutational events happening in the same bacterium is about four in ten million billion ($1 \times 10^{-8} \times 4 \times 10^{-8} = 4 \times 10^{-16}$) cells. An event of such low probability is unlikely to occur even in a large laboratory culture of bacterial cells. With natural selection, cells having both properties are the common result.

The Typing Monkeys and the Painter

Critics have sometimes alleged as evidence against Darwin's theory of evolution examples showing that random processes cannot yield meaningful, organized outcomes. It is thus pointed out that a series of monkeys randomly striking letters on a typewriter would never write *The Origin of Species,* even if we allow for millions of years and numerous monkeys.

This criticism would be valid if evolution depended only on random processes. But natural selection is a nonrandom process that promotes adaptation by selecting combinations that "make sense," i.e., that are useful to the organisms. The analogy of the monkeys would be more appropriate if a process existed by which meaningful words would be chosen every time they appeared on the typewriter; we also had typewriters with previously selected words rather than just letters in the keys; and there was a process for selecting meaningful sentences every time they appeared on this second typewriter. If every time words such as "the," "origin," "species," and so on, appeared on the first kind of typewriter, they each became a key on the second kind of typewriter, then meaningful sentences would occasionally be produced on this second typewriter. If such sentences became incorporated into keys of a third type of typewriter, in which meaningful paragraphs were selected whenever they appeared, it is clear that pages and even chapters "making sense" would eventually be produced.

We need not carry the analogy too far, since it is not fully satisfactory, but the point is clear. Evolution is not the outcome of purely random processes, but rather there is a selection process that picks up adaptive combinations because these reproduce more effectively and thus become established in populations. These adaptive combinations constitute, in turn, new levels of organization upon which the mutation (random) plus selection (nonrandom or directional) process again operates.

As illustrated by the bacterial example, natural selection produces combinations of genes that would otherwise be highly improbable because natural selection proceeds stepwise. The vertebrate eye did not appear suddenly in all its present perfection. Its formation requires the appropriate integration of many genetic units, and thus the eye could not have resulted from random processes alone. The ancestors of today's vertebrates had, for more than half a billion years, some kind of organs sensitive to light. Perception of light, and later vision, were important for these organisms' survival and reproductive success. Accordingly, natural selection favored genes and gene combinations increasing the functional efficiency of the eye. Such genetic units gradually accumulated, eventually leading to the highly complex and efficient vertebrate eye. Natural selection can account for the rise and spread of genetic constitutions, and therefore of types of organisms, that would never have existed under the uncontrolled action of random mutation. In this sense, natural selection is a creative process, although it does not create the raw materials—the genes—upon which it acts.[3]

There is an important respect in which an artist makes a poor analogy for natural selection. A painter usually has a preconception of what he wants to paint and will consciously modify the painting so that it represents what he wants. Natural selection has no foresight, nor does it operate according to some preconceived plan. Rather it is a purely natural process resulting from the interacting properties of physico-chemical and biological entities. Natural selection is simply a consequence of the differential multiplication of living beings. It has some appearance of purposefulness because it is conditioned by the environment: which organisms reproduce more effectively depends on what variations they possess that are useful in the environment in which the organisms live. But natural selection does not anticipate the environments of the future; drastic environmental changes may be insuperable to organisms that were previously thriving.

The team of typing monkeys is also a bad analogy for evolution by natural selection, because it assumes that there is "somebody" who selects letter combinations and word combinations that make sense. In evolution there is no one selecting adaptive combinations. These select themselves because they multiply more effectively than less-adaptive ones. There is, however, a sense in which the analogy of the typing monkeys is better than the analogy of the artist, at least if we assume not that any particular statement was to be obtained from the monkeys' typing endeavors, but only any statements that happen to make sense. Natural selection does not strive to produce predetermined kinds of organisms, but only organisms that are adapted to their present environments. Which characteristics will be selected depends on which variations happen to be present at a given time in a given place. This in turn depends on the random process of mutation, as well as on the previous history of the organisms (i.e., on the genetic make up they have as a consequence of their previous evolution).

Natural selection is an "opportunistic" process. The variables determining what direction it will go in are the environment, the preexisting constitution of the organisms, and the randomly arising mutations.

Interface of Chance and Determinism

Adaptation to a given environment may occur in a variety of different ways. An example may be taken from the adaptations of plant life to desert climate. The fundamental adaptation is to the condition of dryness, which involves the danger of desiccation. During a major part of the year, sometimes for several years in succession, there is no rain. Plants have accomplished the urgent necessity of saving water in different ways. Cacti have transformed their leaves into spines, having made their stems into barrels containing a reserve of water; photosynthesis is performed on the surface of the stem instead of in the leaves. Other plants have no leaves during the dry season, but after it rains they burst into leaves and flowers and produce seeds. Ephemeral plants germinate from seeds, grow, flower, and produce seeds—all within the space of the few weeks while rainwater is available; the rest of the year the seeds lie quiescent in the soil.

The opportunistic character of natural selection is also well-evidenced by the phenomenon of adaptive radiation. The evolution of *Drosophila* flies in Hawaii is a relatively recent adaptive radiation. There are about 1,500 *Drosophila* species in the world. Approximately 500 of them have evolved in the Hawaiian archipelago, although this has a small area, about one twenty-fifth the size of California. Moreover, the morphological, ecological, and behavioral diversity of Hawaiian *Drosophila* exceeds that of *Drosophila* in the rest of the world.

Why should such "explosive" evolution have occurred in Hawaii? The overabundance of *Drosophila* there contrasts with the absence of many other insects. The ancestors of Hawaiian *Drosophila* reached the archipelago before other groups of insects did, and thus they found a multitude of unexploited opportunities for living. They responded by a rapid adaptive radiation; although they are all probably derived from a single colonizing species, they adapted to the diversity of opportunities available in diverse places or at different times by developing appropriate adaptations, which range broadly from one species to another.

The process of natural selection can explain the adaptive organization of organisms, as well as their diversity and evolution, as a consequence of their adaptation to the multifarious and ever-changing conditions of life. The fossil record shows that life has evolved in a haphazard fashion. The radiations, expansions, relays of one form by another, occasional but irregular trends, and the ever-present extinctions, are best explained by natural selection of organisms subject to the vagaries of genetic mutation and environmental challenge. The scientific account of these events does not necessitate recourse to a preordained plan, whether imprinted from without by an omniscient and all-powerful designer, or resulting from some immanent force driving the process toward definite outcomes. Biological evolution differs from a painting or an artifact in that it is not the outcome of a design preconceived by an artist or artisan.

Natural selection accounts for the "design" of organisms, because adaptive variations tend to increase the probability of survival and reproduction of their carriers at the expense of maladaptive, or less adaptive, variations. The arguments of Aquinas or Paley against the incredible improbability of chance accounts of the origin of organisms are good as far as they go. But neither of these scholars, nor any other authors before Darwin, were able to discern that there is a natural process (namely, natural selection) that is not random but rather is oriented and able to generate order, or "create." The traits that organisms acquire in their evolutionary histories are not fortuitous but determined by their functional utility to the organisms.

Chance is, nevertheless, an integral part of the evolutionary process. The mutations that yield the hereditary variations available to natural selection arise at random, independently of whether they are beneficial or harmful to their carriers. But this random process (as well as others that come to play in the great theater of life) is counteracted by natural selection, which preserves what is useful and eliminates the harmful. Without mutation, evolution could not happen because there would be no variations that could be differentially conveyed from one generation to another. But without natural selection, the mutation process would yield disorganization and extinction, because most mutations are disadvantageous. Mutation and selection have jointly driven the marvelous process that, starting from microscopic organisms, has spurted orchids, birds, and humans.

The theory of evolution manifests chance and necessity jointly implicated in the stuff of life; randomness and determinism interlocked in a natural process that has elaborated the most complex, diverse, and beautiful entities in the universe—the organisms that populate the earth, including humans who think and love, endowed with free will and creative powers, and able to analyze the process of evolution itself that brought them into existence. This is Darwin's fundamental discovery, that there is a process that is creative though not conscious. And this is the conceptual revolution that Darwin completed: that everything in nature, including the origin of living organisms, can be accounted for as the result of natural processes governed by natural laws. This is nothing if not a fundamental vision that has forever changed how humankind perceives itself and its place in the universe.

The Teleology of Organisms

Teleology can be defined without implying that future events are active agents in their own realization or that the end results of a process are consciously intended as goals. The notion of teleology arose most probably as a result of our reflection on the circumstances connected with our own voluntary actions. The anticipated outcome of their actions can be envisaged by humans as the goal or purpose toward which they direct their activity. Human actions can be said to be purposeful when they are intentionally addressed toward the attainment of a goal.

The plan or purpose of the human agent may frequently be inferred from the actions the agent performs. That is, the actions can be seen to be purposefully or teleologically ordained toward the realization of a goal. In this sense, the concept of teleology can be extended, and has been extended, to describe actions, objects, or processes that exhibit an orientation toward a certain goal or end state. No requirement is necessarily implied that the objects or processes tend consciously toward their specified end-states, nor that there is any external agent directing the process or the object toward its goal. In this generic sense, teleological explanations are those explanations in which the presence of an object or a process in a system is explained by exhibiting its connection with a specific state or property of the system to whose existence or maintenance the object or process contributes. Teleological explanations account for the *existence* of a certain feature in a system (the configuration of a knife or a bird's wings) by demonstrating the feature's contribution to a specific property (cutting or flying) of the system. The essential element is that teleological explanations require that the property that the feature serves must be *the explanatory reason for the existence of the feature*. Accordingly, it is appropriate to give a teleological explanation of the operation of the kidney in regulating the concentration of salt in the blood, or of the configuration of a bird's wings, given that kidneys evolved precisely because they regulate the composition of blood, and the bird's wings came to be because they serve for flying. But it makes no sense to explain teleologically the motions of a planet or a chemical reaction. In general, as will be shown presently, teleological explanations are appropriate to account for the existence of adaptations in organisms while they are neither necessary nor appropriate in the realm of inanimate nature.

There are at least three categories of biological phenomena in which teleological explanations are appropriate, although the distinction between the categories need not always be clearly defined. These three classes of teleological phenomena are established according to the mode of relationship between the structure or process and the property or end-state that accounts for its presence. Other classifications of teleological phenomena are possible according to other principles of distinction. A second classification will be suggested later.

1. Organisms in which an end-state or goal is consciously anticipated by the agent. This is purposeful activity and it occurs in humans and probably, although to a lesser degree, in other animals. I am acting teleologically when I buy an airplane ticket to Mexico City. A cheetah hunting a zebra has at least the appearance of purposeful behavior. However, as I said above, there is no need to explain the existence of organisms and their adaptations as the result of the consciously intended activity of a Creator. There is a purposeful activity in the living world, at least in humans; but the sheer existence of the living world, including humans, need not be explained as the result of purposeful behavior. When some critics expel the notion of teleology from the natural sciences, they have in mind exclusively this category of teleology.

2. Self-regulating or teleonomic systems, where there exists a mechanism that enables the system to reach or to maintain a specific property in spite of environmental fluctuations. The regulation of body temperature in mammals is a teleological mechanism of this kind. In general, the homeostatic reactions of organisms belong to this category of teleological phenomena. Two types of homeostasis are usually distinguished by biologists—physiological and developmental—although intermediate and additional types do exist. Physiological homeostatic reactions enable the organism to maintain certain steady states in spite of environmental shocks. The regulation of the composition of the blood by the kidneys, and the hypertrophy of muscle in case of strenuous use, are examples of this type of homeostasis.

Developmental homeostasis refers to the regulation of the different paths that an organism may follow in its progression from zygote to adult. The development of a chicken from an egg is a typical example of developmental homeostasis. The process can be influenced by the environment in various ways, but the characteristics of the adult individual, at least within a certain range, are largely predetermined in the fertilized egg. Aristotle, St. Augustine, and other ancient and medieval philosophers took developmental homeostasis as the paradigm of all teleological mechanisms. According to St. Augustine, God did not directly create all living species of organisms, but these were implicit in the primeval forms created by him. The existing species arose by a natural "unfolding" of the potentialities implicit in the primeval forms or "seeds" created by God.

Self-regulating systems of servo-mechanisms built by humans belong in this second category of teleological phenomena. A simple example of such servo-mechanisms is a thermostat unit that maintains a specified room temperature by turning the source of heat on and off. Self-regulating mechanisms of this kind, living or human-made, are controlled by a feedback system of information.

3. Structures anatomically and physiologically constituted to perform a certain function. The human hand, for example, is made for grasping, and the eye for vision. Tools and certain types of machines made by humans are teleological in this third sense. A watch, for instance, is made to tell time, and a faucet to draw water. The distinction between the second and third categories of teleological systems is sometimes blurred. Thus, the human eye is able to regulate itself within a certain range to the conditions of brightness and distance so as to perform its function more effectively.

Teleological mechanisms and structures in organisms are biological adaptations. They have arisen as a result of the process of natural selection. Natural selection is a mechanistic process defined in genetic and statistical terms as differential reproduction. Some genes and genetic combinations are transmitted to the following generations on the average more frequently than their alternates. Such genetic units will become more common, and their alternates less common, in every subsequent generation.

The genetic variants arise by the random processes of genetic mutation and recombination. Genetic variants increase in frequency and may eventually become fixed in the population if they happen to be advantageous as adaptations in the organisms which carry them, since such organisms are likely to leave more descendants than those lacking such variants. If a genetic variant is harmful or less adaptive than its alternates, it will be eliminated from the population. The biological adaptations of the organisms to their environments are, then, the result of natural selection, which is nevertheless a mechanistic and impersonal process.

The adaptations of organisms—whether organs, homeostatic mechanisms, or patterns of behavior—are explained teleologically in that their existence is ultimately accounted for in terms of their contribution to the reproductive fitness of the species. A feature of an organism that increases its reproductive fitness will be selectively favored. Given enough generations it will extend to all the members of the population.

Patterns of behavior, such as the migratory habits of certain birds or the web-spinning of spiders, developed because they favored the reproductive success of their possessors in the environments where the population lived. Similarly, natural selection can account for the existence of homeostatic mechanisms. Some living processes can be operative only within a certain range of conditions. If the environmental conditions oscillate frequently beyond the functional range of the process, natural selection will favor self-regulating mechanisms that maintain the system within the functional range. In human beings, death results if the body temperature is allowed to rise or fall by more than a few degrees above or below normal. Body temperature is regulated by dissipating heat in warm environments through perspiration and dilation of the blood vessels in the skin. In cool weather the loss of heat is minimized, and additional heat is produced by increased activity and shivering. Finally, the adaptation of an organ or structure to its function is also explained teleologically in that its presence is accounted for in terms of the contribution it makes to reproductive success in the population. The vertebrate eye arose because genetic mutations responsible for its development occurred, and were gradually combined in progressively more efficient patterns, the successive changes increasing the reproductive fitness of their possessors in the environments in which they lived.

Inanimate Nature Is Not Teleological

Inanimate objects and processes (other than those created by people) are not teleological because they are not directed toward specific ends; they do not exist to serve certain purposes. The configuration of a sodium chloride molecule (common salt) depends on the structure of sodium and chlorine, but it makes no sense to say that that structure is made up so as to serve a certain end, such as getting food to taste salty. Similarly, the shape of a mountain is the result of certain geological processes, but it did not come about so as to provide slopes suitable for skiing. The motion of the earth around the sun results from the laws of gravity, but it does not exist in order that the seasons may occur. We may use sodium chloride as food, a mountain for skiing, and take advantage of the seasons, but the use that we make of these objects or phenomena is not the reason why they came into existence or why they have certain configurations. On the other hand, a knife and a car exist and have particular configurations precisely in order to serve the ends of cutting and transportation. Similarly, the wings of birds came about precisely because they permitted flying, which was reproductively advantageous. The mating display of peacocks came about because it increased the chances of mating and thus of leaving progeny.

As previously argued, a teleological explanation accounts for the existence of a certain feature in a system by demonstrating the feature's contribution to a specific property or state of the system. Teleological explanations require that the feature or behavior contribute to the persistence of a certain state or property of the system: wings serve for flying; the sharpness of a knife serves for cutting. Moreover, this contribution must be the reason why the feature or behavior exists at all.

The configuration of a molecule of sodium chloride contributes to its property of tasting salty and therefore to its use as food, not vice versa; the potential use of sodium chloride as food is not the reason why it has a particular molecular configuration or tastes salty. The motion of the earth around the sun is the reason why seasons exist; the existence of the seasons is not the reason why the earth moves about the sun. On the other hand, the sharpness of a knife can be explained teleologically because the knife has been created precisely to serve the purpose of cutting. Motorcars and their particular configurations exist because they serve transportation, and thus can be explained teleologically. Not all features of a car contribute to efficient transportation—some features are added for aesthetic or other reasons. But as long as a feature is added because it exhibits certain properties—like appeal to the aesthetic preferences of potential customers—it may be explained teleologically. Nevertheless, there may be features in a car, a knife, or any other man-made object that need not be explained teleologically. That knives have handles may be explained teleologically, but the fact that a particular handle is made of pine rather than oak might simply be due to the availability of material.

Similarly, not all features of organisms have teleological explanations. In general, as pointed out above, those features and behaviors that are considered adaptations are explained teleologically. This is simply because adaptations are features that come about by natural selection. Among alternative genetic variants that may arise by mutation or recombination, the ones that become established in a population are those that contribute more to the reproductive success of their carriers. The effects on reproductive success are usually mediated by some function or property. Wings and hands acquired their present configuration through long-term accumulation of genetic variants adaptive to their carriers. How natural selection yields adaptive features may be explained by examples in which the adaptation arises as a consequence of a single gene mutation. One example is the presence of normal hemoglobin rather than hemoglobin S in humans. One amino acid substitution in the beta chain in humans results in hemoglobin molecules less efficient for oxygen transport. The general occurrence in human populations of normal rather than S hemoglobin is explained teleologically by the contribution of hemoglobin to effective oxygen transport and thus to reproductive success. A second example, the difference between peppered-gray moths and melanic moths, is also due to one or only a few genes. The replacement of gray moths by melanics in polluted regions is explained teleologically by the fact that in such regions melanism decreases the probability that a moth be eaten by a bird. The predominance of peppered forms in nonpolluted regions is similarly explained.

Not all features of organisms need to be explained teleologically, since not all come about as a direct result of natural selection. Some features may become established by random genetic drift, by chance association with adaptive traits, or in general by processes other than natural selection. Proponents of the neutrality theory of protein evolution argue that many alternative protein variants are adaptively equivalent. Most evolutionists would admit that at least in certain cases the selective differences between alternative amino acids at a certain site in a protein must be virtually nil, particularly when population size is very small. The presence in a population of one amino acid sequence rather than another, adaptively equivalent to the first, would not then be explained teleologically. Needless to say, in such cases there would be amino acid sequences that would not be adaptive. The presence of an adaptive protein rather than a nonadaptive one would be explained teleologically, but the presence of one protein rather than another among those adaptively equivalent would not require a teleological explanation.

Evolution as an Open-Ended Teleological Process

There are in all organisms two levels of teleology, *specific* and *generic*. There usually exists a specific and proximate end for every feature of an animal or plant. The existence of the feature is explained in terms of the function or property that it serves. This function or property can be said to be the specific or proximate end of the feature. There is also an ultimate goal to which all features contribute or have contributed in the past— reproductive success. The generic or ultimate end to which all features and their functions contribute is increased reproductive efficiency. The presence of the functions themselves—and therefore of the features that serve them—is ultimately explained by their contribution to the reproductive fitness of the organisms in which they exist. In this sense the ultimate source of explanation in biology is the principle of natural selection.

Natural selection can be said to be a teleological process in a *causal* sense. Natural selection is not an entity but a purely mechanistic process. But natural selection can be said to be teleological in the sense that it produces and maintains end-directed organs and mechanisms, when the functions served by them contribute to the reproductive efficiency of the organism.

The process of natural selection is not at all teleological in a different sense. Natural selection is not in any way directive of the production of specific kinds of organisms or toward organisms having certain specific properties. The overall process of evolution cannot be said to be teleological in the sense of proceeding toward certain specified goals, preconceived or not. The only nonrandom process in evolution is natural selection understood as differential reproduction. Natural selection is a purely mechanistic process and it is opportunistic. The final result of natural selection for any species may be extinction, as shown by the fossil record, if the species fails to cope with environmental change.

The presence of organs, processes, and patterns of behavior can be explained teleologically by exhibiting their contribution to the reproductive fitness of the organisms in which they occur. This need not imply that reproductive fitness is a consciously intended goal. Such intent must in fact be denied, except in the case of the voluntary behavior of man. In teleological explanations the end-state or goal is not to be understood as the efficient cause of the object or process that it explains. The end-state is causally—and in general temporally—posterior.

Three categories of teleological phenomena have been distinguished above, according to the nature of the relationship that exists between the object or mechanism and the function or property that it serves. Another classification of teleology may be suggested attending to the process or agency that gives rise to the teleological system. The end-directedness of living organisms and their features may be said to be *internal* (or *natural*) teleology, while that of manmade tools and mechanisms may be called *external* (or *artificial*) teleology. Objects purposefully designed for a certain function by the actions of an agent have external teleology. Behaviors or actions purposefully performed by an agent seeking certain goals are also endowed with external teleology. A person mowing a lawn or purchasing an airline ticket is acting teleologically, and these actions may also be seen as teleological in the external sense. A lion hunting deer or a bird building a nest exhibit behaviors that seem intentional, and to that extent the results of their actions (e.g., the nest) and the actions themselves may also be considered to be endowed with external teleology.

Internal teleological systems are accounted for by natural selection, which is a strictly mechanistic process. Organisms and their parts are teleological systems in the internal sense; the end-directedness is the result of natural selection. Organisms are the only kind of systems exhibiting internal teleology. In fact they are the only class of *natural* systems that exhibit teleology. Organisms do not possess external teleology. As I have said above, the existing kinds of organisms and their properties can be explained without recourse to a Creator or planning agent directing the evolutionary process toward the production of such organisms. The evidence from paleontology, genetics, and other evolutionary sciences is also against the existence of any immanent force or vital principle directing evolution toward the production of specified kinds of organisms.

It may be useful to distinguish two kinds of natural teleology: *bounded* (or *determinate* or *necessary*), and *unbounded* (or *indeterminate* or *contingent*). Bounded natural teleology exists when a specific end-state is reached in spite of environmental fluctuations. The development of an egg into a chicken is an example of bounded natural teleological process. The regulation of body temperature in a mammal is another example. In general, the homeostatic processes of organisms are instances of bounded natural teleology.

Unbounded design, or contingent teleology, occurs when the end-state is not specifically predetermined, but rather is the result of selection of one from among several available alternatives. The adaptations of organisms are teleological in this indeterminate sense. The wings of birds call for teleological explanation; the genetic constitutions responsible for their configuration came about because wings serve to fly, and flying contributes to the reproductive success of birds. But there was nothing in the constitution of the remote ancestors of birds that would necessitate the appearance of wings in their descendants. Wings came about as the consequence of a long sequence of events, where at each stage the most advantageous alternative was selected among those that happened to be available; but what alternatives were available at any one time depended, at least in part, on chance events.

In spite of the role played by stochastic events in the phylogenetic history of birds, it would be mistaken to say that wings are not teleological features. As pointed out, there are differences between the teleology of an organism's adaptations and the nonteleological potential uses of natural inanimate objects. A mountain may have features appropriate for skiing, but those features did not come about so as to provide skiing slopes. On the other hand, the wings of birds came about precisely because they serve for flying. The explanatory reason for the existence of wings and their configuration is the end they serve—flying—which in turn contributes to the reproductive success of birds. If wings did not serve an adaptive function they would never have come about, and they would gradually disappear over the generations.

The indeterminate character of the outcome of natural selection over time is due to a variety of nondeterministic factors. The outcome of natural selection depends, first, on what alternative genetic variants happen to be available at any one time. This in turn depends on the stochastic processes of mutation and recombination, and also on the past history of any given population. (Whatever new genes may arise by mutation, or whatever new genetic constitutions may arise by recombination, depends on what genes happen to be present—a situation which in turn depends on previous history.) The outcome of natural selection also depends on the conditions of the physical and biotic environment. Which alternatives among available genetic variants may be favored by selection depends on the particular set of environmental conditions to which a population is exposed.

It is important, for historical reasons, to reiterate that the process of evolution by natural selection is not teleological in the purposeful sense. The natural theologians of the nineteenth century erroneously claimed that the directive organization of living beings evinces the existence of a Designer. The adaptations of organisms can be explained as the result of natural processes without recourse to consciously intended end-products. There is purposeful activity in the world, at least in humans, but the existence and particular structures of organisms, including humans, need not be explained as the result of purposeful action.

Some scientists and philosophers who held that evolution is a natural process erred, nevertheless, in seeing evolution as a determinate, or bounded, process. Lamarck thought that evolutionary change necessarily proceeded along determined paths from simpler to more complex organisms.[4] Similarly, the evolutionary philosophies of Bergson,[5] Teilhard de Chardin,[6] and the theories of *nomogenesis*,[7] *aristogenesis*,[8] *orthogenesis*, and the like are erroneous because they all claim that evolutionary change necessarily proceeds along determined paths. These theories mistakenly take embryological development as the model of evolutionary change, regarding the teleology of evolution as determinate. Although there are teleologically determinate processes in the living world, such as embryological development and physiological homeostasis, the evolutionary origin of living beings is teleological only in the indeterminate sense. Natural selection does not in any way direct evolution toward any particular kind of organism or toward any particular properties.

Teleological and Causal Explanations

Teleological explanations are fully compatible with causal explanations.[9] It is possible, at least in principle, to give a causal account of the various physical and chemical processes in the development of an egg into a chicken, or of the physico-chemical, neural, and muscular interactions involved in the functioning of the eye.[10] It is also possible in principle to describe the causal processes by which one genetic variant becomes eventually established in a population by natural selection. But these causal explanations do not make it unnecessary to provide teleological explanations wherever these are appropriate. Both teleological and causal explanations are called for in such cases. Nagel has argued that "teleological explanations are fully compatible with causal accounts. . . . Indeed, a teleological explanation can always be transformed into a causal one."[11] Teleological explanations can be reformulated, without loss of explicit content, to take the form of nonteleological ones. A typical teleological statement in biology is the following: "The function of gills in fishes is respiration, that is the exchange of oxygen and carbon dioxide between the blood and the external water." Statements of this kind account for the presence of a certain feature A (gills) in every member of a class of systems S (fish) that possess a certain organization C (the characteristic anatomy and physiology of fishes). They do so by declaring that when S is placed in a certain environment E (water with dissolved oxygen), it will perform a function F (respiration) only if S (fish) has A (gills). The teleological statement, says Nagel, is a telescoped argument, the content of which can be unraveled approximately as follows: when supplied with water containing dissolved oxygen, fish respire; if fish have no gills, they do not respire even if supplied with water containing dissolved oxygen; therefore, fish have gills. More generally, a statement of the form "The function of A in a system S with organization C is to enable S in environment E to engage in process F" can be formulated more explicitly: "Every system S with organization C and in environment E engages in function F; if S with organization C and in environment E does not have A, then S cannot engage in F; hence, S must have A." The difference between a teleological explanation and a nonteleological explanation directs our attention to "the *consequences* for a given system of a constituent part or process." The equivalent nonteleological formulation focuses attention on "some of the *conditions* . . . under which the system persists in its characteristic organization and activities."[12]

Although a teleological explanation can be reformulated in terms of a nonteleological one, the teleological explanation connotes something more than the equivalent nonteleological one. A teleological explanation implies that the system under consideration is directively organized. For that reason, teleological explanations are appropriate in biology but make no sense when used in the physical sciences to describe natural phenomena such as the fall of a stone or the motion of the planets. Moreover, and most important, teleological explanations imply, as I have argued above, that the end result is the explanatory reason for the *existence* of the object or process which serves or leads to it. A teleological account of the gills of fish implies that gills came into existence precisely because they serve for respiration.

It has been noted by some authors that the distinction between systems that are goal-directed and those that are not is extremely vague. The classification of certain systems as end-directed is allegedly rather arbitrary. A chemical buffer, an elastic solid, or a pendulum at rest are examples of physical systems that appear to be goal-directed. I suggest the use of the criterion of utility to determine whether or not an entity is teleological. The criterion of utility can be applied to both internal and external teleological systems. A feature of a system will be teleological in the sense of internal teleology if the feature has utility for the system in which it exists and if such utility explains the presence of the feature in the systems. Utility in living organisms is defined with reference to survival or reproductive efficiency of the organism itself if such contribution accounts for the existence of the structure or process. Manmade tools or mechanisms are teleological with external teleology if they have utility, i.e., if they have been designed to serve a specified purpose, which therefore explains their existence and properties. If the criterion of utility cannot be applied, a system is not teleological. Chemical buffers, elastic solids, and a pendulum at rest are not teleological systems.

The utility of features of organisms is understood here as having to do with the individual or the species in which the features exist at any given time. It does not mean usefulness to any other organisms. The elaborate plumage and display of the peacock serve the peacock in its attempt to find a mate. The beautiful display is not teleologically directed toward pleasing human beings' aesthetic sense. That it pleases the human eye is incidental, because it does not contribute to the reproductive fitness of the peacock (except, of course, in the case of artificial selection by humans). The criterion of utility introduces needed objectivity in the determination of what biological mechanisms are end-directed. Provincial human interests should be avoided when using teleological explanations, as Nagel has noted. But he selects the wrong example when he criticizes the statement that "the development of corn seeds into corn plants is sometimes said to be natural, while their transformation into the flesh of birds or men is asserted to be merely accidental."[13] The adaptations of corn seeds have developed to serve the function of corn reproduction, not to become a palatable food for birds or humans. The role of wild corn as food is accidental, and cannot be considered to be a biological function of the corn seed in the teleological sense.

The Road Traversed

The Copernican Revolution marks the beginning of science in the modern sense—a commitment to understand the universe as matter governed by natural laws. The Copernican Revolution, however, left out any effort to account for the origin of organisms, with their functional features and endless variations. It was Darwin's genius that brought the living world into the realm of science. Darwin's greatest discovery was natural selection, a process that can account for the origin of organisms and their adaptive features.

I have proposed that the process of evolution, prompted by the interaction between hereditary mutation (a spontaneous, chance process) and natural selection (the differential reproduction of organisms ensuing from their interaction with the environment) may be thought of as a creative process, in the sense that it yields genuine novelty, the myriad organisms with their marvelous features.

Explanatory accounts of the inanimate world are predominantly causal. They seek to identify the antecedent phenomena from which certain necessary consequences follow. Causal explanations apply also to living organisms but are insufficient to account for the teleological aspects of the living world—the undoubtful observation that wings are made for flying, eyes for seeing, and kidneys for regulating the composition of the blood. I have argued that teleology is a distinctive characteristic of the living world and, consequently, that teleological patterns of explanation are indispensable in biology, while they are neither necessary nor appropriate in the realm of inanimate natural processes. It follows that biology cannot be reduced to the physical sciences, although manifesting the autonomy of biology as a scientific discipline has not been the primary concern of this essay.

Notes

1. William Paley, *Natural Theology* (London: Charles Knight, 1936). An argument based on the design of living beings for demonstrating the existence of God was put forward by the French encyclopedist Denis Diderot (1713–1784). In his *Pensées philosophiques,* published in 1746, he argued that only science, and not subjective religious experience, can refute atheism. He saw that evidence for God was apparent in the intricate structure of nature rather than in the vast motion of the universe; that the organization of a seed, a butterfly, or a bird was too complex and precise to have come about by chance. However, Diderot changed his mind a few years later. In *A Letter to the Blind* (1749), he contended that blindness and other birth defects were "monsters" that could hardly be reconciled with the design of a benevolent Creator. See "A Letter to the Blind for Those Who See," in Margaret Jourdain, trans. and ed., *Diderot's Early Philosophical Works* (Chicago: 1966), pp. 113–14. Cited by Karen Armstrong, *A History of God* (New York: Ballantine Books, 1994), pp. 342–43 and 423.

2. Charles Darwin, *On the Origin of Species by Means of Natural Selection* (London: John Murray, 1859).

3. A common objection posed to the account I have sketched of how natural selection gives rise to otherwise improbable features, is that some postulated transitions, for example from a leg to a wing, cannot be adaptive. The answer to this kind of objection is well known to evolutionists. For example, there are rodents, primates, and other living animals that exhibit modified legs used for both running and gliding. The fossil record famously includes the reptile *Archaeopterix* and many other intermediates showing limbs incipiently transformed into wings endowed with feathers. One challenging transition involves the bones that make up the lower jaw of reptiles but that have evolved into bones now found in the mammalian ear. What possible function could a bone have, either in the mandible or in the ear, during the intermediate stages? However, two transitional forms of therapsids (mammal-like reptiles) are known from the fossil record with a double jaw joint—one joint consisting of the bones that persist in the mammalian jaw, the other composed of the quadrate and articular bones, which eventually became the hammer and anvil of the mammalian ear.

4. J.-B. Lamarck, *Zoological Philosophy,* trans. H. Elliot (New York: Hafner, 1809, reprinted 1963).

5. H. Bergson, *L'Évolution créatrice* [1911]; *Creative Evolution,* trans. Arthur Mitchell, republication of the 1911 edition of Henry Holt and Company (Lanham, Maryland: University Press of America, 1983).

6. P. Teilhard de Chardin, *The Phenomenon of Man,* trans. Bernard Wall (New York: Harper Torchbooks, 1959).

7. E. S. Berg, *Nomogenesis or Evolution Determined by Law* (London, 1926; Cambridge: M.I.T. Press, 1969).

8. H. F. Osborn, "Aristogenesis, the Creative Principle in the Origin of Species," *American Naturalist* 68, 1934, 193–235.

9. E. Nagel, *The Structure of Science* (New York: Harcourt, Brace and World, 1961); F. J. Ayala, "Teleological Explanations in Evolutionary Biology," *Philosophy of Biology* 37, 1970, 1–15.

10. I use the "in principle" clause to imply that any component of the process can be elucidated as a causal process if it is investigated in sufficient detail and in depth, but not all steps in almost any developmental process have been so investigated, with the possible exception of the nematode *Caenorhabditis elegans.* The development of *Drosophila* fruitflies has also become largely known, even if not yet completely. The evolution of complex structures has been recently expounded in telling detail by Richard Dawkins in *Climbing Mount Improbable* (New York: W. W. Norton, 1996). He describes, for example, the gradual evolution of the eye of vertebrates. Eyes have independently evolved several dozen times, resulting in organs different in structure and complexity. We should not be surprised to see again and again the evolution of eyes in independent lineages, given that light is such a pervasive environmental factor—adaptations that benefit from light have often been useful to diverse organisms. That so many different ways of adapting to light have evolved is an important instance (like adaptation to the desert) of the interplay between determinism and chance, i.e., between natural selection, mutation, and other processes in the organism's response to environmental opportunities.

11. Nagel, pp. 24–25.

12. ibid., p. 405.

13. ibid., p. 424.

3 | ISLAMIC COSMOLOGY: BASIC TENETS AND IMPLICATIONS, YESTERDAY AND TODAY

SEYYED HOSSEIN NASR

Before beginning a discourse on Islamic cosmology, it is necessary to state that the meaning of the term cosmology in Islamic and other traditional contexts differs profoundly from the meaning given to it in the context of modern science. This difference is of such a nature that one could consider the word "cosmology" to have become a polysemic term since the development of modern cosmology. Traditional cosmologies deal with cosmic reality in its totality, including the intelligible or angelic, the imaginal or psychic, as well as the physical domains. They are applications of metaphysical principles to the cosmic realm.[1] Modern cosmologies, in contrast, despite all the recent changes in modern science and attempts by a number of scientists and philosophers to go beyond the dualism of Descartes, are still based essentially on the Cartesian bifurcation, with the concomitant reduction of cosmic reality to *res extensa* and pure quantity. The result is that the qualitative aspects of the cosmos are reduced to the subjective pole and relegated to the domain of Galileo's secondary qualities where they are considered to be cosmically "unreal" and ultimately reducible to quantity. The consequence of this perspective is that modern cosmologies, which are in reality extrapolations of physics, either exclude the other realms of cosmic reality or consider them to be unreal and reducible to the quantitative, or what can be treated mathematically.

As for Islamic cosmology, needless to say, the many different schools of Islamic thought have produced different cosmological schemes[2] similar in a certain sense to the situation of modern science in which, on the basis of a single philosophy of nature going back to Galileo and Descartes, there is not just one but many cosmological schemes, as a cursory study of the history of modern cosmology reveals. The various Islamic cosmological schemes also all function within a single *weltanschauung* derived from the Islamic revelation and based upon the doctrine of unity (*al-tawhīd*). On the basis of this fundamental philosophy of the nature of things in relation to the Divine Principle and to each other, Islamic thought integrated elements of Greco-Hellenistic, pre-Islamic Persian, and Indian cosmological ideas into its unitary perspective. By the tenth century A.D., Islam had developed the cosmologies which for the past millennium have been essential to its understanding of the cosmos in its totality. By this time it had also constructed the framework for the development of the Islamic sciences of nature and diverse views concerning time, space, motion, cause, finality, purpose, etc.[3] In later Islamic history other notable cosmologies developed, especially that of Ibn 'Arabī and his school[4] which has had great metaphysical and mystical significance during the past few centuries; but as far as the sciences of the cosmos are concerned, the earlier cosmological schemes that received their definitive formulations in the tenth century have remained seminal until today, despite many later reformulations and modifications.

In this summary essay we shall confine ourselves to four major topics elaborated in Islamic cosmology but that are also central to current discussions of cosmology in the West: cosmogenesis, cosmic hierarchy and its relation to vertical and horizontal causality, time and the meaning or purpose of creation, and the processes of nature.

Those who were concerned with Islamic cosmology were naturally also drawn to the question of cosmogenesis and the relation between the cosmos and the Divine Principle with which so many verses of the Quran deal. The Sacred Scripture of Islam, like the Bible, states categorically that God is the creator of the cosmos, as when it states that God is "creator or originator [*fāṭir*] of the Heavens and the earth" (VI; 14). Moreover, the act of creation is identified in the Quran, again as in the Bible and especially in the Gospel of John, with the Word of God. As the Quran states, "when He [God] decrees something He saith [*yaqūlu*] to it 'Be', and it is" (II, 117), the creative act being associated with the verb "say" and hence with the Word.[5]

On the basis of the Quran and numerous sayings of the Prophet of Islam or *Ḥadīth* dealing with cosmogenesis, Islamic thought developed a vast doctrine, or rather sets of doctrines, dealing with the origination of the cosmos. In fact, a subtle vocabulary was developed in Arabic and Persian that corresponded with the different meanings of cosmogenesis, meanings that are all incorporated under the single English word "creation." Was creation in time or beyond time? Was it an ordering or reordering of a previously existing *materia* or did it come from nothing? And if it came from nothing, what does "nothing" mean in this context? These and many other questions caused a nuanced vocabulary to be developed for the discussion of the subject. The lack of similar nuance in the West has certainly contributed to the confusions present in some of the recent discussions on the theological significance of the Big Bang theory.

Already a thousand years ago Ibn Sīnā distinguished between four terms dealing with cosmogenesis:

1. *iḥdāth,* meaning the bringing into being of contingent beings (*mumkināt*), whether they be temporal or eternal. Here, contingency and lack of necessity concerning the ontological status of an existent are emphasized. This distinction is different from the division between temporal and eternal, as the latter term was understood by Ibn Sīnā and other Islamic philosophers and scientists.

2. *ibdāʿ,* meaning the bringing into being without any intermediary of incorruptible and eternal beings, whether these beings be corporeal or not.

3. *khalq* (*āfarīnish* in Persian), the most common term used for "creation." Technically, it means "bringing into being," whether with or without intermediaries, and whether the beings it brings into being are corporeal or not.

4. *takwīn,* the bringing into being of corruptible beings through intermediaries.[6]

Thus clearly defined, these terms became central in the discussion of cosmogenesis, but they were not the only terms of significance. Other schools of thought, especially later Sufism, used alternative terms such as theophany (*tajallī*) and effusion (*fayḍ*) to denote the concept of creation. It is not possible here to discuss the subtle differences among all these diverse concepts of creation and the terms used to denote them. These terms are mentioned here only to demonstrate how Islamic thought has been concerned in the deepest sense with the meaning of cosmogenesis.

In light of the present discussion, the various concepts denoted by these terms can be reduced to four main views within which there have been numerous variations and diverse formulations:

1. The view that to assert that God is the creator of the world means that He is its ontological Principle and that the world is contingent and derives its reality from God.

2. The view that to say that God created the world means that He created the world "in time" from nothing.

3. The view that creation means not a single act, whether it be the bestowing of reality along with time and space or "in time." Rather, there is continuous creation (*creatio continua*) that came to be known as *tajdīd al-khalq fī kulli ānāt*.

4. The view of trans-substantial motion (*al-ḥarakat al-jawhariyyah*), according to which at every moment everything in the cosmos is renewed by new forms being added to already existing objects that then act as matter for the new forms.

The first of these views was defended for the most part by the Islamic Peripatetic (*mashshā'ī*) philosophers, the second by those called (in the West) theologians (*mutakallimūn*) and doctors of the Divine Law, the third by the Sufis, and the fourth by Ṣadr al-Dīn Shīrāzī (*Mullā Ṣadrā*) and the followers of his school known as *al-ḥikmat al-muta'āliyah* ("transcendent theosophy").

Much of early Islamic thought was dominated by the debates between the Peripatetics such as al-Fārābī, Ibn Sīnā, and Ibn Rushd on the one side, and the *mutakallimūn* such as al-Ghazzālī and Fakhr al-Dīn al-Rāzī on the other, concerning the meaning of the creation of the world. This question in Islamic philosophy is known technically as that of *ḥudūth wa qidam*. The *mutakallimūn* were on the side of *ḥudūth,* claiming that God created the world "in time" from nothing, whereas the philosophers, most of whom were also outstanding scientists, claimed that time is one of the conditions of the existence of this world and therefore could not have had any reality before the existence of this world. They were therefore on the side of what came to be known as *qidam,* which means literally the oldness of the world. The philosophers also emphasized the contingent (*mumkin*) character of the universe.[7] In opposition to them, the *mutakallimūn* believed that to point to anything as being *qadīm,* that is, not originated in time, is to detract from the nature of God as being alone *qadīm* in the metaphysical sense.[8]

One of the main accusations of al-Ghazzālī against Ibn Sīnā in his critique of the master of Peripatetics in the former's *Tahāfut al-falāsifah* ("Incoherence of the Philosophers") is that Ibn Sīnā believed in "the eternity of the world," and al-Ghazzālī went so far as to accuse Ibn Sīnā of heresy *(kufr)* because of it.[9] Likewise, Ibn Rushd devoted a good part of his *Tahāfut al-tahāfut* ("Incoherence of the Incoherence") to the refutation of al-Ghazzālī's views on this matter.[10] The well-known debate involving Ibn Sīnā, al-Ghazzālī, and Ibn Rushd, not to speak of many other detailed disputations on this issue between the philosophers and theologians—as one finds in the works of Fakhr al-Dīn al-Rāzī and Naṣīr al-Dīn al-Ṭūsī—attest to the seriousness with which Islamic thought has deliberated upon the meaning of "beginning" as far as the cosmos is concerned.

The current discussions among various modern cosmologists on this question, although held within a very different context, must ultimately deal with the same philosophical issues. The latter cannot be shunned by hiding behind the science involved, precisely because the question of "in the beginning" or *in principio* is not a scientific question as the term science is understood today. There is no way to treat *t* = 0 within the discipline of quantum mechanics except by referring to singularities and boundary conditions. The Islamic discussions on this subject therefore remain very pertinent today, despite the changes in scientific view over the past centuries. Among the most enduring of Islamic teachings is the distinction made by Islamic philosophers—going back to Ibn Sīnā, and not Aristotle, as some have claimed—between the contingent nature of the cosmos and the necessity of the Divine Principle, with only Pure Being having the characteristics of necessity (*wujūb*). Today this assertion of the contingency of the universe continues to occupy the attention of many Christian theologians who are also concerned with modern cosmology.

The notion of the renewal of creation at every instant has been cultivated most of all by the later Sufis. One of the earliest and most eloquent expositions of this doctrine is that of 'Ayn al-Quḍāt Hamadānī, the 12th century Persian Sufi and philosopher,[11] although he did not use the technical term *tajdīd al-khalq fī kulli ānāt,* which owes its origin to Ibn 'Arabī. According to this view, the universe is being destroyed and re-created at every moment by God. Like the two moments of breathing, there is a constant expansion (*basṭ*) and contraction (*qabḍ*) of the universe. At every moment everything returns to the Divine Principle and is then re-created, "returned" and remanifested, because left to themselves, contingent beings would immediately collapse into nothingness. Referring to Quranic verses where there is reference to a new creation (as in Quran, L; 15), expositors of this perspective believe that "new creation" does not refer *only* to God creating a new heaven and earth after the end of this world, but also to the truth that God renews creation at every instant.

There is therefore a *creatio continua,* but in a very different sense from the way in which process theology in the West defines this term. Each moment in the life of the universe is witness to a fresh and new cosmos, re-created by the Divine creative act that repeats itself at every moment. We observe continuity in the world only because of the rapidity of this renewal. But if this renewal were to cease, the cosmos would disappear in an instant. God is not only the originator and sustainer of the cosmos, but its constant creator. Creation is not confined to "the beginning," if we may understand this term in a temporal sense, but applies to every present moment, to every now that is therefore also "in the beginning." Time and eternity meet at every present moment, the now being, in fact, the gate to the eternal. When one thinks of the instantaneous collapse of the state vector and desuperimposition in quantum mechanics that accompany our observation and experience of a phenomenon empirically, one realizes how fecund such a view of creation is for those seeking to make philosophical sense of quantum mechanics beyond the speculative ambiguities and even apparent absurdities that have characterized so many of the interpretations of quantum mechanics since its inception.[12]

Mullā Sadrā's theory of trans-substantial motion, in a manner similar to the already discussed views of the Sufis, conceives of cosmogenesis in relation to every moment in the life of the cosmos rather than to a single "in the beginning," without denying a beginning and end to the existence of the corporeal universe.[13] There is a major difference between the view of Mullā Ṣadrā and that of Sufis such as 'Ayn al-Quḍāt Hamadānī. While for the latter at every moment the universe is renewed and re-created, for Mullā Ṣadrā each state of the cosmos at a particular moment itself becomes matter for new forms that are imposed upon it from above. In the language of Islamic thought, the view of the Sufis is called *labs ba'd al-khal'*, or "dressing [with form] after undressing." The Sadrian doctrine, on the other hand, is called *labs ba'd al-labs,* or "dressing after dressing." Mullā Ṣadrā's doctrine thus relates each moment of the cosmos to what was there before—through substantial motion. This means that in a sense the cosmos is *ḥādith,* or created at every moment, because at any given moment it does not exist in the state that it did a moment earlier. This doctrine may therefore in fact be considered once again as a particular version of *creatio continua.* The doctrine of trans-substantial motion also emphasizes the dynamic nature of the cosmos and its constant becoming, without denying either teleology in the cosmic realm or the immutable archetypes manifested in the cosmic domain.

There have been some independent Islamic philosophers, such as Muḥammad ibn Zakariyyā' al-Rāzī and his teacher Abu'l-'Abbās al-Īrānshahrī, who have emphasized several eternal "principles" (*qudamā'*), including time, in their cosmology and have envisaged the cosmogenic process primarily as a demiurgic one, as in one of the two versions of Plato's cosmology. Such views, however, remained marginal. The major schools of Islamic thought, in contrast, have rejected the idea of time as an "eternal principle." Instead, they have all spoken of the genesis of the cosmos as resulting from the act of a Metacosmic Principle beyond the cosmos and time, whether this genesis be seen "in time" or in principle.

What is important to note is that the four major perspectives stated above, with their numerous variations and interpretations, provide a remarkably rich body of the most perceptive and acute metaphysical, philosophical, and cosmological speculation concerning cosmogenesis, dealing with issues and holding positions all of which are very much alive in current discussions on cosmology.

The contrast of these schools to many contemporary views comes from the fact that the mainstream Islamic cosmologies all agree upon the basic doctrine of a Metacosmic Principle as the originator of the cosmos of which the latter is the creation or manifestation. Or, to put it another way, the cosmos is ontologically dependent upon a Reality beyond itself and is neither *sui genesis* nor self-sustained. Other than that, they differ among each other concerning such basic issues as the meaning of the act of creation in regard to time and the very meaning of "in the beginning."

These cosmologies also differ from each other concerning the revealed doctrine that God created the world from nothing, that is, *ex nihilo* or *min al-'adam*. Like certain Jewish and Christian metaphysicians such as the Kabbalists and Meister Eckhart, certain Muslim metaphysicians such as Ibn 'Arabī consider the *nihil* or *'adam* to lie above existence rather than below it. For the Sufis, *'adam* refers to the celestial archetypes upon which God "breathed" the Breath of Compassion (*nafas al-Raḥmān*) by virtue of which these archetypes became existentiated in outward forms.[14] One could therefore speak in the context of Islamic, as well as Jewish and Christian cosmologies of a more esoteric nature, not only of creation by God but also creation *in* God. In this view the substance of the cosmos "flows" from the Divine Reality without either affecting that Reality or casting a shadow upon its transcendence vis-à-vis the cosmos, while that Reality is also present within every grain of sand by virtue of the existence of that grain.[15] However one may conceive the meaning of *nihil* or *'adam* or "in the beginning," there is no doubt that the dominating schools of Islamic cosmology remain united in their assertion that the Ultimate Reality lies beyond the cosmos that it generates and sustains, and under no condition would any of these schools accept the reduction of all reality to the cosmos, and especially to its empirically and experimentally verifiable dimensions.

The second tenet of Islamic cosmology to which we wish to turn is that of hierarchy. Etymologically, hierarchy (*hiero-arche*) means sacred or divine origin, and the term demonstrates by its very linguistic structure the truth that the doctrine of cosmogenesis on the basis of creation by a Divine Agent necessarily implies hierarchy. It is not therefore accidental that various Islamic cosmological doctrines, as is the case with other traditional cosmologies, are based on the notion of hierarchy, so neglected by the mainstream of Western philosophy since Leibnitz, and denied of necessity in its metaphysical sense by the modern natural sciences, based as they are on the study of a single level of existence, the physical.[16] Hierarchy implies that there are distinct levels of existence or ontological levels in the cosmos and that some are higher than others, higher being determined by closeness to the Source of all being and all qualities.

Some Islamic cosmological schemes, all of which simply reaffirm the Quranic doctrine of universal hierarchy, conceive this "great chain of being," to use the well-known image of Arthur Lovejoy,[17] in ontological terms. Accordingly, God is Pure and Absolute Being, and cosmic beings are so many rungs of the ladder leading to that Absolute Reality. Here Islamic thought is similar to that of Christian theologians and philosophers such as St. Thomas. In fact, Ibn Sīnā, called the "first philosopher of being," was instrumental in systematizing the great chain of being in terms of an ontology that was to influence many of the Schoolmen. Other Islamic thinkers conceived the hierarchy in terms of numerical symbols in a Pythagorean manner, as seen in the *Rasā'il* ("Treatises") of the Ikhwān al-Ṣafā', and still others in terms of degrees of light and darkness, as seen in the teachings of the Master of Illumination (*al-ishrāq*), Shihāb al-Dīn Suhrawardī.

Whatever language and type of symbolism is used, the metaphysical reality is the same. This reality confirms that below the Divine Order there exists the cosmos, which is itself comprised of states of reality standing one "over" the other in a hierarchic fashion. Islamic metaphysics was fully aware that the Ptolemaic model of the world was in fact a visible symbol of this reality and not the *basis* of this reality. Therefore, with the destruction of the Ptolemaic view there was no reason in the Islamic mind for the destruction of the hierarchy, which Ptolemaic astronomy symbolized, in contrast to what one can observe in the West during the Renaissance and the 17th century. In any case, metaphysical principles and the Quranic revelation that contains those principles in revealed form require that below the Divine Essence there be the supreme archetypical world of Divine Names and Qualities. The latter are the principles of the archetypes of all things in the cosmos, and below these falls the intelligible world identified with the angelic world of revelation, itself possessing a vast hierarchy. Below those worlds lies the imaginal world associated also with the psychological realm, and below it is the corporeal itself, consisting of form and matter—this latter term not to be confused with the modern notion of matter, which is quite distinct from the Aristotelian *materia*.

Moreover, each higher level of existence is the principle of the one below and can under no condition be reduced to the lower level. Nor can the level below "evolve" through mere material and temporal processes to the level above, as believed by Darwinists, for whom "above" no longer possesses its traditional meaning. Transformation is possible, but only with the aid of and through the agents of higher levels of existence—as can be seen in the transformation of man's fallen soul until its wedding to the Spirit.[18] Nor can anything become through temporal change other than what it is in principle in the "eternal now." Hierarchy stands therefore thoroughly opposed to reductionism and the attempt to explain everything by reducing it to its material and quantitative components. It also emphasizes the significance of vertical causes in addition to the horizontal in the explanation of phenomena, or considered in their totality and in relation to the whole, rather than as artificially isolated segments of physical reality. Even the red color of the rose—not to speak of the world of life, the psyche and the spirit—cannot be "explained" by being reduced to light waves of a certain length caused by purely "horizontal" causes.

Islamic cosmology remains adamant, through its emphasis upon ontological hierarchy, in its opposition to turning the vertical great chain of being into a horizontal, temporal process that would reduce the higher levels of the hierarchy to the lower. Such a reduction would climax with the picture of a cosmos consisting of molecules and dominated by purely physical forces transforming itself gradually into the spirit of the prophets and saints. The Islamic perspective refuses to take creativity away from God and to surrender it to the world of matter undergoing temporal processes. It sees this latter view as a kind of deification of matter and time, even if the category of divinity and the sacred be denied by those in favor of such reductionism. Islamic thought identifies this perspective as a major philosophical error, one to which Islamic thinkers were sensitive in days gone by and to which they responded extensively and categorically in numerous classical texts.

There is hardly an aspect of the meaning of time not investigated in Islamic thought. Like other types of traditional philosophy, such as those of India, Islamic thought has dealt with historic as well as cosmic time, with physical as well as psychological time, with quantitative as well as qualitative time, with the moment as the unit of time as well as the presence of eternity in the ever-present now.[19] The Quran does not speak of continuous time (*zamān*) but of *waqt*, which can be understood as the instant or moment that is also called *ān* by the Islamic theologians. In the Quranic conception, what appears as continuous time ordinarily experienced and empirically measured, and also the *t* of modern science, are in reality a series of moments each connected to God's creative power and "strung together" in such a way that one experiences time[20] as a continuity, as one does the world. In the deepest sense the Quranic view can be interpreted to mean that what one experiences as time is the constant renewal of the cosmos by God at every moment, which is therefore directly related to the Divine Act. It is this view of time (but not of creation "in time") that was to be emphasized by the *mutakallimūn,* who atomized corporeal objects and space as well as time. As for the Sufis, who call themselves the "son of the moment" (*ibn al-waqt*), they identified each instant or moment with eternity, "now" being the gate to the eternal. Hence the expression "eternal now," which has its equivalent in Western mysticism, Hinduism, and elsewhere.[21]

Islamic cosmology was of course fully aware of time as the measure of motion as understood by Aristotle, whose views were discussed and refined by Islamic Peripatetics such as Ibn Sīnā. Later Islamic philosophers such as Mullā Ṣadrā in fact went so far as to consider the three dimensions of space and time as together constituting the four dimensions of physical existence.[22] Moreover, Mullā Ṣadrā related time to the measurement of trans-substantial motion of the corporeal world rather than the movement of the outer sphere of Ptolemaic or Aristotelian astronomy. These conceptions implied that time was a quantity that could be measured, whether through the movement of the heavens or a change of corporeal bodies.

Islamic cosmologists insisted, however, that time was not only quantitative but also qualitative, the latter kind lying beyond the possibility of measurement in the ordinary sense. While quantitative time could be measured astronomically, there was another kind of time that was real and experienced but not quantifiable. Some Islamic philosophers referred to these two kinds of time as macrocosmic and microcosmic time, or, literally, time associated with the horizons (*al-āfāq*) and time associated with souls (*al-anfus*), without the latter being understood simply as subjective experience. Moreover, higher levels of the cosmos such as the imaginal world were considered to have their own "time" as well as "space."[23]

It is important to note here that for the more metaphysical dimensions of Islamic thought, time has never been considered a linear reality or function, such as one sees in both modern Christian theology and modern science.[24] Rather, time possesses a cyclic nature, but without this idea implying a return of cosmic history to the exact same point after the lapse of a particular period of time. The flow of time is what we might call "hylical," that is, returning to a point that corresponds to a similar point in the previous cycle without being a mere repetition.[25]

In addition, it is important to mention that the refusal to reduce time to pure quantity possessing uniformity that can be measured by purely quantitative means has a major implication for cosmology. Rejection of a uniform and purely quantitative time means the rejection of the idea of uniformitarianism and what is called the theory of nomological universality in modern cosmology. It is totally irrelevant to Islamic cosmology whether the rejection of this claim makes the pursuit of cosmological studies possible or not. What matters is whether this theory is true or not. Islamic doctrines would answer this question in the negative, stating that, in fact, the conditions in various periods in the life of the cosmos differ as does the flow of time and its qualitative effect and significance. They reject extrapolating from knowledge of a small point of the spatio-temporal sequence to encompass vast times and spaces beyond the boundaries of what is known. They would question even the meaning of the phrase "billions of years" and would ask exactly what assumptions one must make about the nature of reality in order to speak of the word "year" in that phrase, and to define it exactly as one does in astronomy for the present period in the life of the cosmos.

Islamic cosmology asserts that one has to prove the hypothesis of nomological universality first, and only then apply it, rather than applying it without validation with the excuse that if we do not do so we cannot study cosmology in the modern scientific sense. There are major philosophical, theological, and scientific issues involved in this issue. These need to be studied and clarified so that one can understand exactly what it is that modern cosmologists are discussing, why there are so many differences of opinion among them, and why views and even accepted models are discarded so rapidly. The insistence of Islamic and other traditional cosmologies upon the qualitative nature of time and cosmic history may in fact be considered a positive challenge to Western cosmologists, and even to certain modern Christian theologians concerned with cosmology, to reexamine and elucidate in all honesty and clarity the assumptions that are made about the nature of cosmic reality upon which they base their speculations, extrapolations, and calculations about the vast expanses of time and space.

There is a famous sacred saying (*ḥadīth qudsī*) in which God speaks in the first person through the Prophet of Islam: "I was a hidden treasure; I wanted [literally loved, *aḥbabtu*] to be known; therefore I created the world so that I would be known." Islam therefore not only believes, as do Judaism and Christianity, that the universe has a purpose and is teleological, but asserts clearly that this purpose is associated with God's Self-knowledge. The purpose of the creation of the universe is the attainment of that state of consciousness that knows God and that principal knowledge itself. Put otherwise, the purpose of the universe is in the deepest sense the attainment of an inner realization that would allow God within and at the center of our being to know Himself through His Self-manifestation. The universe is the Self-disclosure of God. It is a revelation to be understood, and has a meaning that can be "read" by those who possess the "literacy" necessary to read the verses (*āyāt*) of the "cosmic book."[26] From the Islamic point of view, teleological knowledge of the cosmos, far from being useless as claimed by modern science, is the most "useful" of all forms of knowledge of the cosmos because it concerns the very *raison d'être* of the cosmos and of our existence in it. It is a basic part of our vocation here on earth, since such a knowledge leads to the knowledge of God, which is humanity's highest end and entelechy.[27]

Islamic cosmology, therefore, compares the cosmos itself with a revealed book. The science of the book dealing with its weight, size, and the composition of its ink and paper certainly tells us something about the book, but it cannot reveal to us the message written upon the pages of the cosmic text. Islamic cosmological sciences never excluded those types of study that dealt with the quantitative aspects and material analyses of this book, but they never accepted such depictions of the nature of the cosmic book as a complete account of cosmic reality. Its purpose can only be seen by our being able to read the message of the "cosmic text."

Islamic cosmology also emphasized the possibility of knowledge of the presence of purpose in what is observed in nature—not the grand and final purposes, but the more immediate goals and ends that natural processes reveal, especially those dealing with the domain of life. As for the grand purposes and aims of cosmic history, those details are known only to God. What is certain for Islam are two truths: the eschatological realities, which are beyond any form of observational science, and the basic metaphysical truth that God is the First and the Last, as the Quran states, or as Christ asserts in the Bible, "I am the alpha and the omega."

Since the time of Francis Bacon, the strong opposition to teleology in modern science has not shaken the faith of Muslims in a purposeful universe; and Islamic thinkers acquainted with modern science have usually been aware that the announcement of the rejection of all purpose in the cosmos by many scientists is in fact, not strictly speaking, a scientific statement but a statement of faith in a particular ideology. Islamic cosmology would add that the lack of purpose in nature claimed by so many modern scientists is due not simply to the fact that the whole of nature is being observed on the basis of a method that excludes the possibility of a teleological dimension to cosmic reality. Rather, it is the result of the reduction of nature to quantity and the identification of a philosophy based on reductionism, materialism, and scientism with the whole philosophy of the natural world. The creeping back of certain forms of teleology into modern science itself, as, for example, in discussions of the anthropic principle, only confirms in the Muslim mind that even a science that limits itself to the quantitative aspect of cosmic reality will eventually confront the shadow of teleology. It will even show up in that remnant and residue of cosmic reality with which modern science has chosen to be concerned since the 17th century. Once honest science is saved from the prison of reductionist and materialistic ideological confinement, teleology has to be admitted as a reality.

There are many other basic tenets of Islamic cosmology that we do not address in this chapter. What has been said, however, is sufficient to indicate the fact that Islamic cosmology is concerned with issues that are very current for Muslim scientists and thinkers in general. These issues should also be of concern to others interested in the development of cosmology in a civilization such as the Islamic, which, although different from the West, possesses a religion belonging to the same family as Judaism and Christianity and was also heir to the Greco-Hellenistic philosophy and sciences, being itself moreover the generator and propagator of a long scientific tradition. Furthermore, the Islamic tradition is one in which the nexus between cosmology and metaphysics, understood as the supreme science of reality or *scientia sacra,* has never been severed and in which the Cartesian dualism and bifurcation has never taken root.

As more and more philosophers, theologians, and to a certain extent physicists in the West begin to seek a more integrated cosmology and question the Cartesian bifurcation, with its tendency to denude the "objective world" of all qualities, the significance of Islamic cosmology and its relevance for the reconstruction of a holistic cosmology will become more evident. For it can do justice to the full reality of the cosmos with its diverse levels of existence, and it can contribute to the creation of a science that would seek to understand the *esse* of things as well as their mathematical structure. As for the Islamic world, it is only in the context of this wider cosmology that modern Western science can be critically evaluated, transformed, and integrated into the Islamic intellectual universe without sacrificing its own integrity and authenticity.

Notes

1. For an in-depth understanding of the cosmological perspective in the traditional context, see T. Burckhardt, *Mirror of the Intellect,* trans. and ed. W. Stoddart (Albany: State University of New York Press, 1987), pp. 13–16. See

also S. H. Nasr, *Knowledge and the Sacred* (Albany: State University of New York Press, 1989), Chapter 6, "The Cosmos as Theophany," pp. 189–220.

2. On different schemes of Islamic cosmology see S. H. Nasr, "Cosmological Doctrines," in *Islamic Culture,* Vol. IV (Paris: UNESCO, in press). See also A. Bausani, "Cosmologia e religione nell' Islam," *Scientia,* 108, 1973, 723–67; and al-Suyūtī, Jalāl al-Dīn *Islamic Cosmology,* trans. A. M. Heinen (Wiesbaden: Steiner, 1982).

3. We have discussed these cosmologies in S. H. Nasr, *An Introduction to Islamic Cosmological Doctrines* (Albany: State University of New York Press, 1993).

4. On Ibn 'Arabī's cosmology, based on the primacy of the Divine Names the interplay of whose theophanies (*tajalliyāt*) constitute cosmic reality as such, see W. Chittick, *The Self-Disclosure of God—The Principles of Ibn al-'Arabī's Cosmology* (Albany: State University of New York Press, 1997).

5. On Quranic verses dealing with creation see F. Rahman, *Major Themes of the Qur'ān* (Minneapolis: Bibliotheca Islamica, 1980).

6. See L. Gardet, *La Pensée religieuse d'Avicenne (Ibn Sīnā)* (Paris: J. Vrin, 1951), p. 65; and S. H. Nasr, *An Introduction to Islamic Cosmological Doctrines,* pp. 212–13.

7. Similar debates were to take place in Christianity going back to the attacks on the "eternity of the world" by John the Grammarian, who was also well known to Muslim authors, some of whom incorporated certain of his arguments into their writings.

8. There is a vast literature on this subject in both Islamic and European languages. For examples of works in European languages, see H. A. Davison, *Proofs for Eternity, Creation and the Existence of God in Medieval Islamic and Jewish Philosophy* (New York and London: Oxford University Press, 1987); H. A. Wolfson, *The Philosophy of the Kalam* (Cambridge: Harvard University Press, 1976); and D. B. Burrell and B. McGinn (eds.), *God and Creation* (Notre Dame: University of Notre Dame Press, 1990).

9. See al-Ghazālī, *The Incoherence of the Philosophers (Tahāfut al-falāsifah),* trans. M. E. Marmura (Provo, Utah: Brigham Young University Press, 1997).

10. See Ibn Rushd, *Tahāfut al-tahāfut,* trans. S. van den Bergh (Cambridge: Gibb Memorial Trust, 1987), the first four discussions, pp. 1–170.

11. See T. Izutsu, "The Conception of Perpetual Creation in Islamic Mysticism and Zen Buddhism," in *Creation and the Timeless Order of Things* (Ashland, Oregon: White Cloud Press, 1994), pp. 141–73.

12. Wolfgang Smith has already dealt with this relation in his profound work, *The Quantum Enigma* (Peru, Illinois: Sherwood Sugden, 1995), especially Chapter 6, "In the Beginning," p. 99ff.

13. On Mullā Sadrā and the doctrine of trans-substantial motion see S. H. Nasr, *The Islamic Intellectual Tradition in Persia* (London: Curzon, 1996, pp. 271–303; and S. H. Nasr and O. Leaman (eds.), *History of Islamic Philosophy* (H. Ziai), Chapter 35, "Mullā Sadrā: His Life and Works," pp. 635–42, and S. H. Nasr, Chapter 36, "Mullā Sadrā: His Teachings," pp. 643–62.

14. On the metaphysical significance of *ex nihilo* see F. Schuon, *The Play of Masks* (Bloomington, Indiana: World Wisdom Books, 1992), *"Ex nihilo, in Deo"*, pp. 37–42. As for the concept of the "Breath of the Compassionate" in relation to the creation of the cosmos, see S. H. Nasr, *Science and Civilization in Islam* (Cambridge: Islamic Text Society, 1987, and New York: Barnes and Noble, 1992), p. 344ff.

15. For an extensive treatment of this subject see L. Schaya, *La création en Dieu* (Paris: Dervy-Livres, 1983).

16. On the centrality of this doctrine in traditional metaphysics and cosmology, see H. Smith, *Forgotten Truth* (San Francisco: HarperSanFrancisco, 1993), p. 34ff. On the role of this central doctrine in Western thought see P. G. Kuntz (ed.), *The Concept of Order* (Seattle and London: University of Washington Press, 1968), and H. Krings, *Ordo: Philosophische-historische Grundlegung einer abendländishen Idee* (Halle: M. Niemeyer, 1941).

17. See his classical work, *The Great Chain of Being* (Cambridge: Harvard University Press, 1936).

18. One can of course use the symbol of depth rather than height and speak of more inward rather than higher, ultimately considering the Divine Principle as the Immanent rather than the Transcendent. But if correctly understood, such an Immanent Reality cannot but also be the Transcendent. Without acceptance of the transcendent dimension, immanentism can become readily reduced to a philosophical pantheism, which can then easily "harmonize" itself with modern materialistic cosmologies, as can be seen in so many expressions of "New Age" religions.

19. For a discussion of diverse theories of time in both East and West, see K. Vatsyayan (ed.), *Concepts of Time—Ancient and Modern* (New Delhi: Indira Gandhi National Centre for the Arts, 1996). There are several articles in this work about the Islamic conception of time.

20. See L. Massignon, "Le temps dans la pensée islamique," *Eranos Jahrbuch*, 20, 1952, 141–48.

21. For a masterly summary of this traditional doctrine see A. K. Coomaraswamy, *Time and Eternity* (New Delhi: Indira Gandhi National Centre for the Arts, 1990).

22. Some contemporary Islamic thinkers have been drawn to comparing this view with that of Einstein in his theory of relativity. See Ḥ. 'A. Rāshid, *Daw fīsūf-i sharq wa gharb, Ṣadr al-muta' allihīn wa Einstein* (Isfahan: Ta'īd Press, 1953/54).

23. See H. Corbin, *En Islam iranien,* Vol. I (Paris: Gallimard, 1971), p. 177ff.

24. See Abu Bakr Siraj ed-Din, "The Islamic and Christian Conceptions of the March of Time," *Islamic Quarterly,* 1, 1954, 229–35.

25. See H. Corbin, *Cyclical Time and Ismaili Gnosis,* trans. R. Mannheim and J. Morris (London: Kegan Paul International, 1983).

26. I have dealt with this issue in several of my books, such as *Science and Civilization in Islam,* p. 337ff.

27. A contemporary Christian theologian formulates the attitude of modern science toward teleology as follows: "For the most part scientific thought still avoids any suggestion that questions about the purpose of things lead us to true or useful knowledge." John F. Haught, *Science and Religion: From Conflict to Conversation* (New York: Paulist Press, 1995), p. 166. Traditional Islamic thought would respond that knowledge of final causes or purpose of things is true knowledge of the highest order as far as knowledge of the cosmos is concerned as well as being of the greatest "use" to man after knowledge of God which, as already stated, is the final purpose of the creation of the cosmos itself.

4 | COSMOS AND CONSCIOUSNESS: INDIAN PERSPECTIVES

ANINDITA NIYOGI BALSLEV

T he contemporary concern for removing the hard boundary between religious and scientific thought can, perhaps, draw a number of helpful insights from ancient Indian culture. Undoubtedly, one of the most pertinent ways of initiating a conversation between science and religion is to ask about the relationship the idea of *cosmos* might have with that of *telos*. It is also fruitful, of course, to explore various ideas that deal with the origin and nature of the universe, that is, with cosmogony and cosmology. Not only is there available to us an enormous amount of material on origins, cutting across cultures from an early time in history, but the relevant documents can be said to belong to an epoch of human inquiry when the hard boundaries of disciplines that divide science and religion today had yet to be invented.

However, instead of detailing the scientific achievements that have occurred in the Indian context, some of which are generally known, I would prefer to look closely into Indian thought to recapture that holistic sense—encompassing the question of both cosmology and teleology—with which we are now apparently losing touch. If we feel unreconciled to our present conceptual situation, it is precisely because we fail to understand the legitimacy of the intellectual struggle for a meaning that our religious consciousness demands. It is therefore not surprising that some modern scientists writing on cosmology also seem to be groping with the question of purpose in the universe, in its physical as well as biological aspects. As we look at some of the Indian philosophical sources bearing on these issues, we shall perceive how they weave the topics of cosmology and teleology into a conceptual whole.

In this connection, one may well wonder whether there is any serious difference between the Indian and the Western cultural traditions that can account for the manner in which science and metaphysics have been evaluated in each case. Only after dealing with this question shall we be in a position to examine the extent to which any such differences may have actually influenced the respective contentions about how far apart the objectives of these disciplines are.[1]

To pinpoint a major difference, I refer to a few statements contained in the synopsis setting forth the theme of this conference on cosmology and teleology. The central question for discussion is whether an "overarching purpose can be attributed to the universe." What is entailed in the notion of "purpose" as well as that of "universe" by scholars of various disciplines? To explore the question of *telos,* it seems to me that it is not enough to accumulate information about the material universe alone. We also need to direct our attention to the theme of consciousness. The primacy of consciousness, at least in the epistemic or evidential sense, is undeniable. I emphasize this point by saying that in thinking about the question of purpose, a given conceptual framework may have a meaning without our having to postulate the idea of "creator," but it cannot do so without our taking into account the "knower" of the cosmos. The cosmos is an object of knowledge for us, and cosmology—in all of its various models—is constituted by human consciousness. Consciousness provides the ultimate testimony to the fact that anything at all exists, enabling us to say that it is thus and not otherwise. As the ancient Indian philosophers said, the "darkness of the world" (*jagadandhaprasanga*) will proceed without that minimal assumption. To say all of this, however, is not the same as claiming the ontological priority of consciousness. (Regarding this last question, various philosophical possibilities are explored and recorded in the histories of both Indian and Western philosophy.)

Now, to make a long story short, the immediate philosophical response to the question of cosmic purpose in the Indian context will generally be that the *jada,* or the nonconscious, cannot be said to *have* any purpose of its own (especially when the conceptual scheme allows for a dualistic metaphysics where both matter and consciousness are seen to be on a par as ontological categories). Whereas the material/physical universe can of course be seen as serving a purposeful function for the conscious agent, the question of metaphysical purpose arises only in the case of that which is conscious. I will come back to this point later, after discussing briefly some of the relevant ideas pertaining to cosmology from the Indian sources.

For the moment, I would like to remark that in such statements as the one made by Steven Weinberg,[2] that "the more the universe seems comprehensible, the more it also seems pointless," or that human existence in this universe seems to be a "farcical outcome," the author's own implicit presuppositions about the presence of consciousness in the universe are not made sufficiently explicit. Had his views appeared in a metaphysical treatise, the author would be held accountable for such unexamined assumptions. My point is that, while struggling with the issues of *cosmos* and *telos,* we need to be apprised, for example, of when physicists begin to play the role of metaphysicians—unaware of their doing so—or when theologians, for that matter, attempt arbitrarily to set limits to the kind of inquiry undertaken by the present-day cosmologist.

With these few remarks as a preamble, I will delve straight into the subject matter of my essay, which is to show how the concerns about *cosmos* and *telos* are tied up in Indian thought. There are very early documents, no later than 1500 B.C., that record the Vedic seer asking, "*kutah ayam visrsti?*" ("Wherefrom this creation?") Thus, the beginning of cosmogony in the Indian context can be traced from here in the *Rig Veda* itself, where the idea of an ordered universe is clearly expressed in the notion of "*rta*" (order). What is significant for our present discussion is that this idea of "*rta*" has a double import. "Order" is understood here in such a way that it could be expressed both in terms of the law of the uniformity of nature and that of the moral order. It is this latter interpretation that subsequently found expression in the pan-Indian concept of the law of *karma,* stressing the efficacy of human actions. "We cannot escape the law of *karma* any more than we can escape the law of gravity"—as Basham has observed.[3] This is not understood as fatalism, since one can utilize knowledge of the law to guide one's life. It is based on the intuition that the idea of an occurrence of an event without a necessary dependence on anything else is unacceptable, be it in the natural or in the moral sphere. In these ideas the notion of causality, which will later appear as a central problem in Indian thought, is already in the making. The *Upanishads* breathe an atmosphere wherein there is a definite groping for a principle that creates, regulates, sustains, and controls all there is. Here we come across a record of intensive speculation leading to a rejection of all those views that advocate spontaneous, haphazard, arbitrary origination, and emphasizing instead that the contingent must have a cause. Here the idea of causality can be dispensed with only with regard to that which is discerned as "never-present" or "ever-present."

From the period of the *Upanishads* onwards, we can recapitulate briefly some of the basic features of Indian thought up to our own day. Of capital importance is the idea that "being cannot come out of nothing" (*nasato' vidyate bhavo*), an idea that all schools of Indian philosophy share. This principle is to remain a prominent aspect of Indian cultural reasoning, and various schools of Indian philosophy later demonstrated the sort of logical absurdities to which a transgression of the principle *ex nihilo nihil fit* can lead. This fundamental assumption has had a strong impact on both soteriology as well as cosmology.

Thus, in speculating about the origin of the universe, we must rule out any idea that the universe could emerge from nothing. However, even in the case of theistic considerations, the position that an almighty God could "create" this world *ex nihilo* (technically called *isvaravada*—God-ism) was rejected by some theists themselves, principally because in that case God alone would be responsible for all the disparities among living beings. The differences (*vaisamya*) that are evident right from the moment of origin would have to be attributed to God alone, and consequently God could be charged with being partial and cruel. In other words, the concept of God as entailing not simply arbitrary power but power inter-woven with justice, mercy, compassion, etc., has historically played an important role in Indian cosmological reflection. As a consequence of these considerations, classical Indian thought never ascribes an absolute beginning to the world process. Despite all the variations in its cosmologi-cal models, the tradition adheres to the notion of *anadi-samsara*—the position that the world process is without a beginning. This holds true also of the nontheistic schools of thought within the pale of Brahmanism, Buddhism, and Jainism, which otherwise offer their respective views about cosmos, *karma,* and salvation without postulating a personal god.

Interestingly, however, although no idea of an absolute beginning is admitted, the notion of repeated creation and dissolution of the world process is abundantly present in Indian thought. This idea, which has its earliest documentation in the *Rgveda Samhita,* can be found not only in the *puranas* and the epics, but also in the literature of various other schools of Indian thought. Although this model, mentioned above, is the predominant one, I would also note that there was another cosmological model that did not entertain the idea of periodic dissolution. It simply accepted the world process as having no beginning, insisting that the world had never been otherwise (*na kadacit anidrsam jagat,* as the school of Mimamsa claimed).

As examples of systematic and rigorous thinking about nature in the ancient Indian context, mention must be made especially of the *Sankhya (yoga)* and the *Vaisesika (Nyaya)* schools. Interesting theoretical contrasts show up in their accounts of the process of nature's unfolding. *Sankhya* works within a conceptual frame in which the dominant idea is that of cosmic evolution, whereas *Vaisesika* operates within the framework of an atomic theory, projecting the view that there are basic constituents that unite in a mechanical manner. These ideas, combined with divergent views about space, time, and causality, were offered as theoretical accounts of the manifold of experience with which we are all familiar. The two schools also exemplify how both nontheistic and theistic frameworks fashion ideas about the mode of operation of natural processes. In each case, attempts are made to comprehend the linkage between consciousness and cosmos.

For *Sankhya*, the unfolding of the whole course of the universe is an interplay of two principles: *prakrti*, the ever-changing, ever-active principle of matter, and *purusa*, the principle of consciousness (an idea modeled after the Upanishadic notion of *atman*) as unchanging and unchangeable, uncaused and indestructible. The manifested world, in this conceptual frame, is traced to an unmanifested ground where nature (*prakrti*) is conceived as composite—a tri-unity of the three *gunas* (*sattva, rajas,* and *tamas,* representing the three tendencies in the material principle, viz. inertia, action, and manifestation). Nature is said to be uncaused and indestructible. In its empirical aspect, it is in a state of equilibrium (*samya-vastha*) in which the *gunas* have not yet begun to combine; hence it is described as formless and undifferentiated.

It is important to note that intertwined with the notion of cosmic evolution is the idea of cosmic dissolution. Eventually the universe will disintegrate and return to the original state of that equilibrium in which the state of uniform, equal diffusion of the *gunas* leads to homogenous modification (technically called *sadrsa-parinama*), i.e., a state in which these do not combine and hence no new evolution can occur. In the unequal aggregation of the *gunas* (which occurs in the evolution of nature), there is a constant tendency to return to the original stable state, a state in which the evolutionary process is arrested until the commencement of a fresh creative cycle.

In the metaphysical pluralism of the *Vaisesika* system, the ultimate constituents of the empirical world are said to be atoms (*paramanunu*)—its material cause. The philosophical accounts of production, destruction, etc. are different from that of the dualistic school of *Sankhya.* Despite their common point of departure in upholding the notion of a world process without a beginning, these two schools came up with different views of time and causality.[4] For the *Vaisesika,* the contingent entity is necessarily an effect, interpreted as a new "beginning" (*arambha*) of that which was not there before the causal operation brought it about (hence, the theory is termed *Asatkaryavada* in Sanskrit).

Note that for the thinkers of this school the beginning of an effect, i.e., the occurrence of a contingent entity, is an event-in-time. Further reflection led the school to put forward the view of an absolute time. The ontological features of this idea of time *per se* were carefully noted: it is said to have no beginning or end, since the beginning or ending of any event presupposes time. Time is further characterized as all-pervasive, indivisible and unitary. A distinction was made between the idea of absolute time (*mahakala*)—time *per se*—and the relative, conventional time (*vyavaharika kala*) that allows for a pluralistic usage of time. Thus, all conventional intervals of time—divisions such as a moment, an hour, a day, a month, or a year, etc.—are made possible by the use of any standard motion, of which ordinarily the solar motion is the most dominant. For those who shared this position it was universally thought that without postulating the objective reality of an absolute time we would be confronted with a static universe where nothing occurred.

It is notable that this "event-in-time" conception is conspicuously absent in the literature of *Sankhya,* held to be the oldest school of Indian philosophy. According to *Sankhya,* an account of the phenomena of change and becoming, or for that matter a philosophical explanation of the conventional uses of the three time-phases, viz. past, present, and future, does not necessitate the concept of an empty time as an ontological category. Change needs to be understood, the literature says, in the light of the *Sankhya* theory of causality (technically called *satkaryavada*). In this context, unlike in *Vaisesika,* an effect is perceived not as an entirely new beginning but as an actualization of that which was potentially existent prior to the causal operation. As a result, the so-called time-order is woven into the texture of transformation to which a thing is subject, that is, in its changing from being potential to actual, and from the actual to the sub-latent. Thus the three phases of time are accounted for in the following way: the present is the mark of actuality, the future the mark of potentiality, and the past that of sub-latency. The Yoga school makes much out of this idea, claiming that the whole universe can be said to undergo transformation in one single moment, which is the real/actual time. "No two moments can be said to exist simultaneously." Hence, any notion of a collection of moments or of an objective sequence is nothing but a conceptual construct. This is one of the several versions of discrete time that one can find in the Indian philosophical literature.

The Indian views of the cosmos as bound by laws that one cannot override are connected with these widely divergent views about time and causality (the other views cannot be treated in the compass of this short chapter, but see note 4). However, none of these ideas about the cosmos are devoid of moral or soteriological implications. On the contrary, delving deep into these ideas opens us up to that conceptual arena masterfully occupied by the *puranas,* the great body of literature constituting Indian mythology, weaving intimate stories of human significance into the backdrop of cosmological cycles spanning billions of human years.

At this point it may be useful to comment on the prevalent cliche that the Indian view of time is "cyclical" in contrast to the Judeo-Christian understanding of linear time. This misconception is largely the result of a failure to see the inter-connections between philosophical views, religious ideas, myths, and symbols about time; it is also the consequence of a misreading of the notion of cosmic cycles that I have already mentioned. For example, there is no mechanical recurrence of specific phenomena or of human destiny, as some have thought. Moreover, a simplistic metaphorical designation as "cyclical" or "linear" cannot be taken to be an adequate representation of any major thought tradition. Just as in the history of Western thought one comes across a number of views where some advocate the view of absolute time and others say that time is a relation or a process, there are several positions regarding time in the history of Indian thought, some of which I have noted above.

Another idea found across cultures is that time is mere appearance with no ontological reality. This notion is also present in Indian thought. The school of *Advaita Vedanta,* for example, in its zeal to establish philosophically that consciousness is the sole ontological reality, reduced the problem of time *qua* change to a problem of appearance. The result is that cosmology in this philosophical context has only epistemic status. Hence, any quest for understanding cosmic purpose involves a comprehension of how consciousness is conceived by the various schools. The complexity of this search increases as one adds to the Brahmanical positions—those mainly discussed in this paper—other views expressing similar concerns stemming from the Buddhist and the Jaina traditions as well.

In fact, to appreciate the overall ethos of Indian culture, one has to take into account not only ideas concerning the vastness of time, but also such views as that of "many worlds," a number of which are even said to be inhabited. These ideas, however difficult it is to trace their origins, are part and parcel of Indian religious discourse. What is startling is that ancient Indian thinkers could weave a network of ideas wherein a greater knowledge about the physical world was not seen in any way as antithetical to the religious quest.

Occasionally in current literature one comes across opinions that claim that earlier articulations of religious meaning all assumed a narrow sense of space and time, or that prior to our own age there were no cosmic ideas comparable in scope to the modern scientific conception of an ever-expanding universe and the possible existence of other inhabited planets.

This view can be considerably chastened by a knowledge of the network of ideas that constitute the Indian conceptual world. It seems to me that a remarkable feature of Indian thought is the integration of its religious, scientific, and metaphysical ideas into a coherent and cosmically expansive holism.

A sense of the vastness of space and time, instead of hampering an earnest soteriological quest, can instead augment it. In one of several recorded conversations that the nineteenth-century Indian saint Sri Ramakrishna had with his visitors—as documented in the *Gospel of Sri Ramakrishna*—he compares the countless worlds with the innumerable crabs on the sandy beach in a rainy season.[5] His purpose was that of instilling a sense of humility and inspiring an urgency for the spiritual quest in one of his interlocutors. His point was that the knowledge of the immensity of the universe and the plurality of worlds does not make the search for a religious meaning redundant. The cultivation of such a broad attitude is inspired by a holistic approach that can do justice to both religious and scientific enterprises. This way of looking at ourselves and the vast universe is surely an outstanding contribution of Indian culture. We should also be clear that if a scientist today, operating within the theoretical framework of his or her discipline, finds the universe to be "pointless" or "pitilessly indifferent to human beings"—a notion to which this conference draws our attention—this must be taken as an attitude demanding philosophical scrutiny. Such a declaration entails a complex set of assumptions that perhaps remain unexamined and not yet articulated by the scientist in question. A reductionist view of consciousness, as we know from the Indian sources, can find no other purpose but the pursuit of pleasure as the *summum bonum* of human life. This view was recommended by the *Carvaka* philosophers on the basis of a philosophical materialism for which consciousness is no more than an epiphenomenon. It is one of many possible scenarios that can be drawn from reflection on our own presence in this vast universe.

However, a perusal of the global history of ideas reveals other proposals, some of which we have received from various philosophico-religious traditions. These seem to have the advantage of providing us with a sense of dignity and direction, suggesting alternative ways of comprehending our presence and purpose. Despite all the admirable knowledge that we now have of the physical and the biological universe, there is no obvious reason why a scenario that openly fails to perceive any meaning or purpose in human existence should claim our loyalty more than the other alternatives accessible to us. There is nothing philosophically more compelling about interpretations of the universe that fail to see any such purpose, especially when the conceptual assumptions behind such views are not brought clearly to the surface for our consideration.

I can only repeat, then, that any response to the question of "an overarching purpose" to the cosmos is inseparable from the view one takes with respect to consciousness, in the context of both life and death. In the Indian world several such positions have emerged. For the materialists death is taken to be the extinction of consciousness, and so fulfillment of hedonistic goals is seen as the only purpose of life. Sometimes while examining such positions from the viewpoint of scientific cosmologies, in which human life is pictured as a meaningless accident, one cannot help feeling that they are based on specific contentions regarding the origin and status of human consciousness that need to be made more explicit. Moreover, one can even wonder why—accepting that human life (or, for that matter, life as such) is nothing more than an accident—this position could not at least foster an attitude where "insentient nature," which has provided a set of physical circumstances congenial to the occurrence of such an "accident," could be seen as something other than a source to be ruthlessly exploited. Fruitful debates and discussions can take place only on the premise that all hidden assumptions should be brought to the surface.

It is also becoming more and more evident that a deeper sense of the current ecological crisis will lead to the search for a theology of nature, and consequently for a sharpening of our sense of the relationship between consciousness and insentient nature. In the Indian context, there are records of interesting arguments as to why consciousness cannot be said to be derived from a nonconscious principle. Consequently, there are philosophical schemes that make room for both matter and consciousness, as we have noted in the case of *Sankhya* and *Vaisesika*. There are also positions in which consciousness is declared to be the only ontological reality, as in *Advaita Vedanta,* where the empirical world has only epistemic status. According to this view, the highest goal of human life lies in obtaining the knowledge of the self (*atman*), which is the goal of the pursuit of salvation. This position illustrates how deeply a view of consciousness can affect ideas about the purpose of human life or that of the universe. The notions of salvation (for which the Brahmanical, Jaina, and Buddhist terms are *moksa, kaivalya,* or *nirvana*) can be seen as tied to different modes of conceiving consciousness. Attitudes to nature and to all sentient beings are influenced by these same readings. This world is an abode of experience—a *bhogasthana,* as it is said in Sanskrit—for all sentient beings. All sentient beings make use of this physical and biological universe for various purposes. Human beings alone are aware of the distinction between this-worldly pursuits and the religious quest for salvation.

In this connection, an issue of theological interest is that some Indian thinkers thought that the very idea of fulfillment of a purpose presupposes a sense of want, a lack of some sort, that is felt by an agent in question. This is also why, in the theistic context, they were hesitant to say that there is a divine purpose behind the universe, inasmuch as God cannot be said to have any lack. Instead, they developed the notion of divine play or sport *(lila)*.

Finally, why are we undertaking the quest for understanding the relationship of cosmology to teleology? It is surely not because we are seeking to comprehend only views about the cosmos from the standpoint of specific religious traditions such as Hinduism or Islam or Christianity. Nor is it because we are expecting to find answers to such questions in the material with which present-day advanced scientific cosmology is equipped to provide us. It is, rather, that we hope to detect the presuppositions that underlie those readings of science that claim that the universe is "pointless"—readings allegedly based on *scientific* cosmology.

Note that here the term "scientific" is no longer descriptive, but is a value-laden term. And, like many others, I find the philosophical presuppositions of such statements to be questionable, not to mention their inability to satisfy our religious yearning—a dimension of human existence that we just do not seem to be able to abandon. A religious view of the universe not only places before us a challenge to consider the point of our own lives, but it also constantly provokes us to think twice before engaging in ruthless and careless exploitation of the natural world. In this respect, an important function of those thought traditions that attribute an ethico-religious dimension to the universe is not simply to provide empirical information about ourselves and our habitat. As a challenge to reformulate the goal and purpose of human life, they are a constant call to restructure our own values as well.

To be religious, however, is not to be unscientific. And to be scientific is not the same as being committed to a doctrine of philosophical materialism. Once we arrive at a framework of knowledge free of unproductive and unwarranted discussions and disputes between science and religion, we will feel free to strive for further insight into the as-yet unexplored secrets of the universe. And, at the same time, we shall be able to pray, as in the *Upanishads:* "Lead me from the unreal to the real, from darkness to light, from death to deathlessness."[6]

Notes

1. "For the Indian metaphysician, science and metaphysics remain continuous: both undertake to study the structure of the world, and they differ only in the order of generality. . . . One reason why, in traditional western metaphysics, the metaphysical scheme claimed a sort of necessity over against those features of the world which the sciences study is that metaphysics and science have stood sharply separated ever since the beginning of metaphysics in Aristotle." (J. N. Mohanty, *Reason and Tradition in Indian Thought* [New York: Oxford University Press, 1992], p. 233).

2. Steven Weinberg, *The First Three Minutes: A Modern View of the Origin of the Universe* (New York: Basic Books, 1976).

3. A. L. Basham, *The Wonder That Was India* (London: Sidgwick & Jackson, 1987).

4. For more on this topic, see my *Study of Time in Indian Philosophy* (Otto Harrassowitz: Wiesbaden, 1983), and co-editor, *Religion and Time* (Leiden: E. J. Brill, 1993).

5. *The Gospel of Sri Ramakrishna,* trans. and introduction by Swami Nikhilananda (New York: Ramakrishna-Vivekananda Center, 1952).

6. From the *Brhadaranyaka Upanishad.*

5 | COSMOLOGY, SCIENCE, AND ETHICS IN JAPANESE NEO-CONFUCIANISM

MARY EVELYN TUCKER

Introduction

I would note at the outset that while Confucianism does not posit an overarching teleology, as do other religious traditions, it clearly affirms moral purpose in the universe. This is evident in its understanding of nature and the role of humanity in relation to nature. Briefly described, the Confucian and Neo-Confucian traditions[1] envisage the vast interacting universe as organic, dynamic, harmonious, and morally purposeful. By "organic" I mean that there is an affirmation of natural process; by "dynamic" I am suggesting that there is an affirmation of change and pattern; by "harmonious" I mean that there is an affirmation of reciprocal resonance; and by "morally purposeful" I am indicating the traditions' affirmation of the universe as profoundly meaningful.

While there is no doctrine of creation *ex nihilo* in the Confucian tradition, there is certainly an understanding of an ongoing creative process at the heart of the natural world.[2] This dynamic creativity is expressed as both pattern and change. Change is celebrated as the continual transformative nature of the universe and as the source of the fecundity of life. At the same time, pattern and connectivity are taken to be imprints of meaningful relations woven throughout the fabric of natural and human life. Underlying the essential Confucian quest for harmony is the establishment of relational resonance between nature and humans. This is evident in the early classical texts, especially the *I Ching* (*Book of Changes*). The interrelation of heaven, earth, and humans is to be continually realized through patterns of correlative thinking and rituals of correlative reciprocity.[3] Within this cosmology, nature is seen as in process and meaningful. While the idea of an overarching purpose or teleology is not present in the tradition, there is certainly a sense, not unlike *contemporary process thought,* of purposive events within the flow of nature.[4] Indeed, the notion of the Tao as the Way or Path indicates that there are profoundly meaningful dimensions to the universe. The myriad things in nature do not arise without pattern and purpose. Instead, Confucianists say, they emerge from the interaction of yin and yang, the primal pair of opposites in the universe. The Confucians thus view the universe as morally purposeful. It is the task of humans, therefore, to interact with the patterns of nature and bring harmony to human affairs.

Given this understanding of Confucian cosmology—as organic, dynamic, harmonious, and morally purposeful—what can we say regarding the reception of Western science in such an intellectual context? Here I will concentrate on the case of Japan rather than become entangled in the complex debates sparked by Joseph Needham and others regarding the lack of mathematically based experimental science in China.[5] I will first survey the historical situation of premodern Japan during the Tokugawa period (1603–1868) when Western science first entered Japan. Then I will discuss two important "natural scientists" in Japan during the seventeenth and eighteenth centuries, Kaibara Ekken and Miura Baien. For both of them, nature was morally purposeful, so they tried to hold their empirical and ethical concerns in creative tension. I would suggest that their interest in the material force *(ch'i)* of the universe may have important implications for contemporary efforts to foster a postmodern science as suggested by Steven Toulmin, Frederick Ferré, and others.

I am using the term "empirical" in this essay to describe, in a broad sense, the investigation of nature. I am not assuming contemporary scientific or empirical methods of research, but rather the study of nature frequently attributed to naturalists. (Mathematically based experimental science was a phenomenon that arose first in the West.) In the same sense, then, I am using the term "science" to describe the efforts of various Neo-Confucians to investigate principles within the material world. One of the most fascinating questions in the study of Confucianism is why the imperative of Chu Hsi to explore principles "without" (and abide in reverence "within") never developed in the direction of a scientific method such as that which arose in the West. Nonetheless, Japan was quite open to various types of science (especially medical) and adapted both Chinese and Western ideas to its own needs.[6]

Japan's Premodern Period

During the Tokugawa period Japan experienced certain political, social, economic, and educational circumstances that conditioned the entry of Western science. This was a period of unification and peace after many years of civil war at the end of the sixteenth century. The emperor was a symbolic figurehead in Kyoto, while real political power was concentrated with the Shogun in Edo (Tokyo). To secure the borders and maintain internal stability, the Tokugawa Shoguns sealed off the country from outside influences and forbade Japanese who were abroad from returning. This closed country policy, known as *Sakoku,* included a prohibition on the importation of Western books. The only concession to external contacts was to allow the Dutch to establish a trading post on an island in Nagasaki harbor. The prohibition was partially lifted in 1720 by Shogun Yoshimune. From that time forward, Dutch books were permitted and Dutch studies, known as *Rangaku,* began to flourish, especially in the field of medicine. However, there were still attempts to control learning through the office of the Shogun in Edo, especially in the Prohibition of Heterodoxy in 1760.

Tokugawa society was organized into four classes with samurai at the top, followed by farmers, artisans, and merchants. Merchants were at the bottom because profit-making was traditionally looked down upon by the educated class (literati) in East Asia. However, during this period trade began to flourish, especially along the eastern coastal road known as *Tokaido.* As the rice markets of Osaka grew, so did trade with the Shogun and with the *daimyo* (provincial lords) in residence in Edo. Trade increased as the *daimyo* traveled to Edo along the *Tokaido* road to fulfill the Shogun's order to remain in residence there for three-year intervals. The Shogun instituted this as a means of controlling the political and military ambitions of the *daimyo.*

During this period members of the samurai class were making a transition from warriors to civil servants and educators. While some of them remained masterless and unemployed *ronin,* many found employment as educators or advisors to local *daimyo.* The learning promoted by these samurai was significant in both extent and diversity. *Daimyo* were instructed and their children educated. Schools were established and people of different classes were taught.[7] A number of types of Confucianism flourished, including Chu Hsi (Jp. *Shushi*), Wang Yang-ming (Jp. *Oyomei*), and the Ancient Learning School (*kogaku*).

It was in this context that various forms of Western science were imported into Japan during the Tokugawa period, including medical studies, astronomy, mathematics, and botany. Questions arise then as to how they were received and about what kinds of premodern science (especially studies of nature) might have emerged in this period.[8] First, let us note that the rise of science in the West is often associated with a research methodology combining the ideals of empiricism and objectivity with a world view regarding nature as operating by mechanical and measurable principles. This understanding of science has frequently resulted in some kind of struggle and split with revealed religion. In Japan, however, this was not the case, as the Confucian intellectual tradition was relatively tolerant of new ideas and perspectives. Moreover, this tradition did not hold revealed truths in scripture or orthodox theologies regarding creation. Thus, scientific ideas such as heliocentrism and evolution did not arouse the same suspicion and opposition they did in the West.

There were other political and social factors that promoted science in Japan, such as the peace and stability established by the Tokugawa government. The constant travel within Japan to and from Edo encouraged the exchange of ideas. Moreover, the government on both local and national levels patronized scholarship, supported libraries, promoted publishing, and established schools. The Shogun founded several scientific institutions, including the Astronomical Bureau and Observatory, the Translation Office, and the Academy of Western Medicine. Numerous private schools and about 23 medical academies arose during the period. The port of Nagasaki remained a significant center where books from China were imported, and even some works from the West found their way into Japan despite the prohibition on foreign books.

Some growth of science was inhibited, however, by the seclusion policy that could encourage parochialism and discourage the dissemination of knowledge. Moreover, intellectually the development of science was impeded by certain aspects of Confucianism regarding the method and content of learning. For example, Confucianism tended to promote loyalty of students to teachers and thus frequently did not encourage individual curiosity or creativity. It emphasized the memorization of texts and the importance of tradition rather than innovation.

In addition, there was a lack of appreciation of mathematics by the Confucians, who saw numbers as connected to the merchant class and profit-making. Hence, a mathematically based scientific method was difficult to develop within Japan. Moreover, an approach to learning that was simply technical or quantifiable was far from the aim of the Confucians. Even practical learning (*jitsugaku*) was intended to benefit the people and be undertaken in the context of a vibrant Confucian cosmological framework.[9] Research apart from this framework was considered trivial or manipulative.

In conclusion, then, while there were factors in Confucianism that both helped and hindered the development of science in Japan, it cannot be said that Confucianism discouraged science from arising there. Rather, what should be noted is that because Confucian thought is based on a cosmological world view, many Confucians accepted science as a philosophy of nature. However, because the Confucian cosmological world view is organic, dynamic, harmonious, and morally purposeful, Confucians did not wish to remove this element from their observations of nature or their studies of the human body. Instead, they sought to maintain a balance between the two poles suggested by Chu Hsi, namely, investigating things without and abiding in reverence within. Thus, the empirical and the ethical were held in creative tension. This is especially evident in the two significant Japanese Neo-Confucian thinkers, Kaibara Ekken and Miura Baien.

Kaibara Ekken

Biography and Intellectual Development

Kaibara Ekken (1630–1714) was born in Chikuzen on the Japanese island of Kyushu.[10] His father, a physician to Lord Kuroda, taught him medicine at home. Although he appreciated Buddhism as a youth, when he was fourteen his interest in the Chinese classics began to grow under the tutelage of his elder brothers. When he was twenty-six he left for Tokyo to become a physician.

Two years later he went to Kyoto to investigate Chinese Confucianism in greater depth. There he studied the thought of Chu Hsi with well-known scholars such as Kinoshita Junan (1621–1698), Nakamura Tekisai (1629–1702), and Yamazaki Ansai (1618–1682). Chu Hsi (1130–1200), one of the greatest thinkers of China, was known as the primary synthesizer of Neo-Confucian thought. The *Four Books,* namely, the *Analects, Mencius,* the *Great Learning,* and the *Doctrine of the Mean,* became the basis for the civil service examination system that lasted for more than 800 years in China.

During these years Ekken also studied the work of the Chinese Neo-Confucian thinkers Lu Hsiang-shan (1139–1193) and Wang Yang-ming (1472–1529). However, after reading the attack of the Ming Confucian Ch'en Chien on these thinkers he rejected their ideas as being too Buddhistic. This critique implied that they were too subjective. Ekken also disliked the excesses of some of Wang Yang-ming's followers. Thus in 1660, at the age of thirty, he became an ardent advocate of Chu Hsi's thought. His feeling for Chu approached a religious reverence. He wrote, "I respect him as if he were a god and I believe in him as one might believe in oracle bones."[11] He published selections of Chu's Chinese works with punctuation marks so they could be read by the ordinary Japanese. He also wrote the first Japanese commentary on Chu's masterful synthesis, *Reflections on Things at Hand (Chin-Ssu Lu)*.

By the time he was forty Ekken had read widely in the Chinese sources, including the early classical Confucian and the later Sung, Yuan, and Ming Neo-Confucians. He was especially influenced by the Ming Confucian Lo Ch'in shun (1465–1547) and eventually embraced his philosophy of *ch'i*. He praised Lo as follows:

> Only Master Lo honored the Ch'eng brothers and Chu Hsi as his teachers without subscribing uncritically to their views. His opinions should be considered most correct and appropriate. There is no Confucian scholar to compare with him in the Yuan and Ming periods. He must be rewarded as a truly distinguished scholar.[12]

Yet, like Lo, Ekken came to have growing reservations about Chu Hsi's thought. He felt it relied too heavily on Buddhist and Taoist sources, which emphasized emptiness. He also felt that its stress on self-cultivation tended to be too quietistic. Ekken set forth these reservations in his treatise *Grave Doubts (Taigiroku)*. It was clearly difficult for Ekken to disagree with Chu Hsi or to make a complete break with his thought. For these reasons, *Grave Doubts* was not published until after his death. In addition to the intellectual debt he felt toward Chu Hsi, Ekken wished to avoid being identified with the Ancient Learning School, mentioned above, which was highly critical of Chu Hsi.

As the Japanese Confucian scholar Okada Takehiko pointed out, Ekken might be best understood as having established a reformed Chu Hsi Confucianism.[13] Okada felt that Ekken derived much of his sensitivity toward nature from Chu Hsi and other Sung thinkers.[14] This reverence toward nature became the primary motivating force in the development of Ekken's own type of practical learning (*jitsugaku*).

Practical Learning: Content and Methods

Ekken's practical learning was broad and comprehensive, spanning both the humanities and the sciences. It was aimed at both moral cultivation and the alleviation of social problems. His scholarly interests touched a wide variety of fields, including "ethics, manners, institutions, linguistics, medicine, botany, zoology, agriculture, production, taxonomy, food, sanitation, law, math, music, military."[15] He was moved by Chu Hsi's directive to "investigate things" and "explore their principle." He wrote: "True scholarship attempts to explain the principles behind phenomena, thus deriving an understanding of them. Without this explanation, the inquiry, no matter how far reaching and detailed, will be worthless."[16]

Although exploring principles remained a primary goal of Ekken's investigations, his method was also indebted to Chu Hsi's instructions to his students at the White Deer Grotto. These included:

1. Value broad learning and wide experiences.
2. Do not be overly credulous but remain skeptical with regard to doubtful cases.
3. Be fair and objective in one's judgments.
4. Investigate thoroughly and reflect carefully before making a judgment.[17]

Ekken described the unacceptable ways of scholarly study as follows:

> One should not blindly regard all one has heard as true and reject what others say merely because they disagree, nor be stubborn and refuse to admit mistakes. To have inadequate information, to be overly credulous about what one has seen and heard, to adhere rigidly to one's own interpretation, or to make a determination in a precipitate manner—all these four modes of thinking are erroneous.[18]

With regard to the need for broad knowledge, Ekken wrote, "The ancients said that all things under the sun are their province and I too must become a man to whom the principles governing all things in the wide world are known."[19] What is particularly striking about Ekken's breadth was his conscious effort to include knowledge pertinent to the ordinary Japanese of this day. His scholarly studies were not limited to textual exegesis or scientific analysis, but they embraced popular culture as well. Indeed, he felt it was his mission to study everyday customs at the same time that he was transmitting Confucian values to the ordinary person.

Ekken was, nonetheless, keenly aware of the importance of maintaining objectivity and rationality in analyzing principles. He was not interested only in collecting data or in becoming a specialist or a technician of knowledge. He wished to bridge the gaps between what we would call the humanities and the sciences and specialized research and popular education. Perhaps Ekken's greatest achievement along these lines was his attempt to develop investigative or empirical studies as part of his religious world view rather than as something completely distinct from it. While his success here may be debated, the importance of his attempt can hardly be lost on the modern reader. To encourage "scientific" studies that do not objectify nature as something apart from the human is one of Ekken's major contributions to the history of Tokugawa thought.

The Ethical and the Empirical Paths:
Bridging the Humanities and the Sciences

Like many Confucians before him, Ekken warned against the limitations of methods used by both the humanist scholar and the scientific researcher. For him, Confucianism as an essentially ethical path had to be distinguished from the textual studies or technical skills as ends in themselves. He urged scholars to maintain a reflective and contemplative mode when exploring the classics so as not to fall into the traps of linguistic analysis and empty exegesis. Similarly, he critiqued the scholarly specialists who were concerned only with personal recognition, and the technicians who were obsessed with manipulative processes. As Okada notes, Ekken felt that "To forget about the cultivation of the moral sense (*giri*) within one's own heart and to seek after worldly success was the way of a specialist, and that to attempt to discover techniques to penetrate into the principle underlying all things was the work of the technician."[20] Hence, in terms of a curriculum of education, he sought to bring together both the humanities and the sciences. He advocated a practical learning that would foster self-cultivation while also assisting others. He urged that learning should be "reserved in the heart and carried out in action."[21] Traditional humanistic values as well as technical skills should be used for the benefit of self and society. In this way the scholar can realize the traditional Confucian aspiration to participate in the transforming and nourishing processes of heaven and earth.

To weld together humanistic and scientific concerns, Ekken believed that a physician should practice humaneness while helping to "nourish life." His skills could not be utilized fully without an understanding of his larger ethical role. Similarly, to study horticulture or to cultivate plants only because of their beauty was to trivialize their larger role in nature. By being concerned with manipulative processes of cultivation, one could fall into the danger of "trifling with things and losing one's sense of purpose."[22] Rather, horticulture and agriculture ought to be undertaken with an understanding of "the proclivity of nature to give birth to living things."[23] An appreciation of nature's mysterious fecundity as the source of life is critical to Ekken's practical learning.

Finally, at the heart of his effort to unify the humanistic and scientific modes of learning was his idea of the unity of principle (*li*) and the diversity of its particularizations. An important extension of this idea was his notion of the constancy of principle along with its transformations. Thus while principle was a unified source of value in human society, it was similarly the source of order in the natural world. Yet at the same time, principle was manifested in a diversity of forms and in a myriad of transformations. Both continuity and change were embraced by principle. The elucidation of this idea became a motivating force of his own form of practical learning.

Because Ekken, following Lo Ch'in shun, collapsed the distinction between principle (*li*) and material force (*ch'i*), his practical learning (*jitsugaku*) was directed toward finding principle within the transformations of material force itself. In terms of moral cultivation this meant that there was no distinction made between one's original heavenly nature and one's physical nature. He saw them as essentially the same, and therefore one's original nature was to be sought within one's own mind and heart (*kokoro*). This same monism could be applied to the natural world to undertake empirical studies uncovering the principle within material force.

The Creative Principles of Filiality and Humaneness

Ekken's practical learning was inspired not only by the monism of *ch'i* but also by his doctrine of humaneness (*jen*) and filial piety (*ko*) as extended to the natural world. From the Neo-Confucian Chang Tsai's doctrine of forming one body with all things, Ekken developed his unique understanding of participating in the transforming and nourishing powers of heaven and earth. While other Confucians saw filiality as having a counterpart in the human and natural worlds, Ekken took this even further by underscoring the need for humans to activate a filial reverence for nature.

A primary motive in this activation of filiality was a sense of the debt of humans to heaven and earth as the great parents of us all. He wrote: "All men may be said to owe their birth to their parents but a further inquiry into their origins reveals that men came into being because of nature's law of life. Thus all men in the world are children born of heaven and earth, and heaven and earth are the parents of us all."[24] Ekken acknowledged the importance of loyalty and reverence to one's parents as the sources of life. He extended this feeling of respect to the entire cosmic order, and maintained that since nature was the source and sustainer of life, one should respond to it as to one's parents, with care, reverence, and consideration. Indeed, persons should serve nature as they would their parents in order to repay their debt for the gift of life. He urged humans to cherish living things and to avoid wantonly killing plants or animals. This concern for nature was a motivating force behind his own scientific research, for he saw it as connected with filiality.

Central to his doctrine of a cosmic filial relationship is an all-embracing humaneness that he defined as "having a sense of sympathy within and bringing blessings to men and things."[25] His scientific and spiritual pursuits were further connected by his understanding of a direct correspondence between humaneness in persons (Ch. *jen;* Jp. *jin*) and the origination principle in nature (Ch. *yuan;* Jp. *gen*). Indeed, he argued that the operation of principle in the Supreme Ultimate (*T'ai chi*) had the unique purpose of creating the myriad things and thus could be termed "the heart of nature" (*tenchi no kokoro*).[26] Just as birth and origination are the key attributes of the natural world, so was humaneness a central characteristic of human beings. Origination was the counterpart in nature as humaneness is in persons. He wrote of the significance of this unique identity of cosmic and human virtues:

> The heart [and great virtue] of heaven and earth is *sei*, becoming . . . What is becoming? (or birth) Shushi [Chu Hsi] said, 'Heaven nourishes or gives life to things. Heaven does nothing but nourish all things.' This is becoming. Then how are we to obey and not to oppose heaven and earth? By benevolence, men receive the nourishing heart which belongs to heaven and earth and make it their own. This is benevolence. Nourishing and benevolence are different aspects of the same thing. Nourishing belongs to heaven and earth, benevolence belongs to man.[27]

The creative processes of the universe find their richest expression in the creative reciprocity of human beings. The fecundity of nature and the wellsprings of the human heart are seen as two aspects of the dynamic activity of change and transformation in the universe. He observed that humans have a harmonious energy granted by nature and that this principle governs human life. "Just as plants and trees continue to sprout without ceasing, so too the 'life force' thrives within us and the heart is made eternally glad—this is happiness."[28] When expressed toward others, this was the creative virtue of humaneness.

For Ekken, then, the human was the "spirit of the universe" and had both great privileges and responsibilities in the hierarchy of the natural world. He wrote, "It is great fortune to be born a human; let us not fritter away our lives meaninglessly."[29] One can avoid doing this by studying the classics, investigating principle, and activating humaneness. He also added the directive to "follow the example of nature" in achieving inner wisdom and contentment. With great detail he described the seasonal changes with which one should harmonize one's own moods and activities. He saw this as participating in the process of transformation, which was the key to both knowledge and moral practice for humans. He wrote:

> Every year without failure the four seasons come to give life to all. The faithfulness of Heaven and Earth is very precious and to be reverenced. Happy are they who meditate on, feel and enjoy the truthfulness of heaven for to them is given the key to all knowledge.[30]

Briefly stated, then, these are some of the central ideas in Ekken's thought:

1. Filial piety is coextensive with the whole natural order.
2. Humaneness is profoundly creative and generative and corresponds to the origination principle in nature.
3. Humans are the spirit of the universe and as such they participate in the transforming and nourishing processes of heaven and earth.

With Ekken we have arrived at the threshold of a scientific methodology dynamized by a Neo-Confucian religiosity. The understanding of the cosmic dimensions of reverence in many Neo-Confucian thinkers is now transformed into a reverent investigation of nature. Similarly, the cosmic filiality of Nakae Toju and other Neo-Confucians was seen as a reason for both protecting and studying nature. Let us turn, then, to Miura Baien to see how these concerns become a more self-conscious drive to articulate a scientific approach to reality.

Miura Baien

Miura Baien (1723–1789) might be viewed as one who carried on Kaibara Ekken's explorations of the natural world. As we have seen, one of Ekken's primary motives in his empirical studies was his strongly religious belief in the familial connection between the human world and heaven and earth. Studies of nature became a means of expressing one's filial duty and of activating the creative virtue of humaneness (*jen*) in the human realm.

Baien, while being less overtly religious, nonetheless maintained strongly Confucian values at the root of his empirical studies. Indeed, the central goal of his research was to "benefit the people" and thus to contribute to the advancement of human relationships.[31] Furthermore, like Ekken, he held that we had a debt to heaven and hoped to provide a means of cooperating with the transformative powers of heaven and earth. He wrote: "In order not to impair things given by heaven one has to aim at helping along the creativity of nature according to each one's status and ability. Doing so they would not go against the great virtue of heaven and earth."[32]

One of Baien's most significant contributions to the advancement of empirical thought was his adamant insistence that while the human can only be understood in relation to nature, we must see nature in its own terms and not simply project anthropomorphic ideas onto it. Wishing to make a clear break with more mythical and animistic ways of representing nature, he wanted to describe nature's own inherent dynamics. For Baien this became a lifelong pursuit, taking the form of an epistemological method that he believed provided a "key for opening the gates of Heaven."[33] His was a pursuit that was both religious and rational, ethical and empirical.

Biography and Intellectual Development

Miura Baien (1723–1789) was born, like Ekken, the son of a physician in Kyushu. His ancestors had originally come to Kyushu from Kamakura at the beginning of the thirteenth century. Although he was the fifth of six children, he was the only son to survive. His father wanted him to continue in his footsteps as a local physician, and because of this Baien refused all offers of employment outside his native fief.

In 1738 he began to attend the provincial school fifteen kilometers away. He studied there from age fifteen through nineteen with a prominent Confucianist scholar Ayabe Keisai (1676–1750), who had been a student of Ito Togai and Muro Kyuso. During this period Baien also went twice to study with the Confucian scholar of the Nakatsu fief, Fujita Keisho. Fujita was so impressed with Baien's learning that he invited Baien to succeed him as the resident Confucian scholar. Baien refused in deference to his father's wishes. At the age of twenty-three he visited Nagasaki, where he made his first contacts with the Dutch scholars of his day. Five years later he went to the principal Shinto Shrine at Ise to pay his respects to the mythical ancestral gods of Japan. Baien was apparently married twice before his third wife bore him a child.[34] He had two sons and two daughters with her. As is recorded in his poetry, he apparently felt great affection toward her and remembered her in his will.

Baien's interests extended to the political and economic spheres and he has been compared to Adam Smith.[35] In 1756 he drew up the regulations for a credit union to assist the local peasants. It was sustained by small, regular contributions from which the farmers could obtain a loan when in need. While he had strong words for those who were poor due to laziness, he had great sympathy for those who were in difficulty because of natural disasters, sickness, old age, or lack of heirs to assist them. It is said that many thousands of people benefited from this association, the results of which have lasted until recent times. His support for farmers was recorded when he was having difficulty getting his *Deep Words (Gengo)* published, and the farmers collected money to be used for its publication.[36]

In 1766 Baien wrote regulations for his school, which again revealed his highly disciplined yet egalitarian views. While the rules of conduct were necessarily strict, it was said that Baien never resorted to corporal punishment to enforce discipline. He insisted on the basic equality of his students and would not permit distinctions due to social status. His only means of rank was by date of entry into the school and by scholarly achievements. He felt the students should be free to choose their teacher and also free to leave when they wished.

He was a traditional Confucian with regard to emphasizing the fundamentally moral nature of education. He thought that learning ought to foster moral behavior (*shushin osameru*). He also taught that it should affect an inner transformation that could nourish one regardless of praise from others: "Learning is both food and it is a spirit which is to be fostered. It is meant to fill our interior and not to be an external embellishment for display in society."[37] While Baien had a limited number of students, they did much to spread his influence.

In 1778, with a group of twelve students (including his son), he set out on his second trip to Nagasaki. This trip was important in terms of contact with Western scientific thought. From the records of the trip, certain of Baien's attitudes, often termed "scientific realism" or "empiricism," emerged clearly. While he believed that the universe had neither a beginning nor an end, he was fascinated with other stories of creation. He saw the Biblical story of Adam and Eve as comparable to the Japanese creation myth of Izanagi and Izanami, who also lost their original pristine quality. He felt that the Western division of the week into seven days was an arbitrary human-made device that did not correspond with the true nature of heaven.

There is some debate over Baien's adherence to a heliocentric view of the universe. Gino Piovesana, however, seems to doubt the validity of such claims, although he notes that the Copernican theory was indeed entering Japan at this time.[38] More significant, however, was Baien's belief in the sphericity of the earth, in contrast to the Confucian notion of heaven as round and the earth as square. He was deeply influenced by Asada Goryu (1734–1799), the foremost Japanese astronomer of his day. In letters to Goryu he seemed to express his puzzlement with the theory of a heliocentric universe, but in *Deep Words* some of his diagrams have the sun at the center. It does seem clear, in any event, that he was quite interested in Western science, especially astronomy.

It is important to note that Western science, especially through Dutch learning, was making an impact on Japan during the eighteenth century. Indeed, several of Baien's colleagues and followers studied Western science at the Kaitokudo in Osaka. It is also true that Baien, like Fang I-chih in seventeenth-century China, lamented the lack of interest in science by many of the Confucians and the over-concern of Western scholars of pragmatic details while ignoring moral concerns.[39]

Baien spent the last ten years of his life in his native village, and it is said he refused Matsudaira Sadanobu's request, shortly before his death, to serve in the Bakufu government. Baien died quietly on the morning of April 11, 1789. It was one of the ironies of his life that a year after his death, Matsudaira Sadanobu issued the "Prohibition Against Heterodoxy," which discouraged promotion of thought other than Chu Hsi Confucianism, especially at the official academies and *han* schools. This may have prevented Baien's ideas from getting a wider reading after his death.[40]

The Creativity of Nature:
Continuities and Discontinuities in Baien's Thought

Miura Baien was both rationalistic and religious, seeing his empirical probings as a means of simultaneously understanding the universe and knowing the will of heaven.[41] While his thought is considered unique and original, it is nonetheless motivated by some of the most enduring concerns of Confucians in both China and Japan.

Baien was, like the Chinese Sung Neo-Confucians, preoccupied with the nature of change in the universe, seeing it as real and not insubstantial, as the Buddhists saw it. He believed that change was the source of the creative forces of nature and sought to explore this as a way to understand how the human can assist the creative process. He was clearly deeply influenced by the *Book of Changes* and the ideas of the circularity of movement and the fusion of opposites found there.[42] Like the Sung masters before him, he spoke of the "creativity of nature (*zoka*) which makes flowers bloom, children to be born, and produces fish and birds."[43] This, he felt, was what should cause both wonder and doubt in the human as regards our own role: "Should man have real concern about himself, there ought to arise some doubts about the heavenly rotations and the creativity of nature."[44] Yet we overlook these things by force of habit. What he wanted in particular was to generate a fresh perspective on nature through more careful observation of its operations.

He celebrated the creativity of heaven as its great virtue, which "generates things ceaselessly."[45] The challenge for humans was to see themselves as assisting in this transformative process: "In order not to impair things given by heaven one has to aim at helping along the creativity of nature according to each one's status and ability. Doing so they would not go against the great virtue of heaven and earth."[46] These points are made at both the beginning and the end of his letter to Taga Bokkyo, one of his students. The student had been inquiring about Baien's teaching on the dialectics of nature, but before Baien answered the student he wanted to clarify the purpose of these observational explorations into nature's activities.

Baien was not only in the tradition of Confucians before him; he was, no doubt, influenced by his contemporaries. He most likely read Yamaga Soko, who wrote: "In everything in Heaven and Earth, in man and things there is but the logic (*jori*) of nature. This is the principle (*li*)."[47] While Soko saw principle in more conventional terms within the Chu Hsi tradition, Baien broke with Chu Hsi's dualism of principle (*li*) and material force (*ch'i*). Like Ekken, he adopted a monism of *ch'i* more in line with Chang Tsai's thought on the creativity of *ch'i*. Also, like Ekken, Baien spent many of his early years in a state of doubt, until at the age of thirty he had a breakthrough in which he "first recognized that heaven and earth is *ch'i*."

Thus, there is a sense of continuity with the past in Baien's thought, while at the same time the claim for his originality cannot be overlooked. Part of Baien's unique genius was to develop an empirical method that relied on a logical dialectic (*jori*). While his particular form of dialectical reasoning has not endured, what is significant is his contribution to fostering the dialectical process as a means of discovering empirical truth and perceiving the patterning in the natural world. The impact of this in eighteenth- and nineteenth-century developments in Japan still remains to be explored.

A New Perspective for Investigation of the Natural World

Baien himself realized that he was breaking new ground in his attempts to develop an empirical method that would reveal the logical structure of reality. He was not worried about criticism he might face, but only spoke of the tenacity with which he pursued his objectives:

> The theory of logic, even in the distant past, has not been developed by any of the ancients. There has not been any kind of introductory work in this area consequently, the thing seems all the more painful.

From my youth I have ruined my teeth on it, and my hair has grown thin. But for all my efforts and pain I myself understand nothing but a part of it. However, applying myself for a lifetime I hope to finally achieve a satisfactory formulation.[48]

Baien's struggle to discover a theory of logic was driven by a radical dissatisfaction with the approach of many of his contemporaries to the study of nature. He wrote:

Though their evidence may be flimsy and their arguments preposterous, this does not disturb people at all. Yet I cannot content myself with this. I keep reconsidering such matters and probing further into them.[49]

Baien's significant restatement of an appropriate empirical method began with an urgent call to view the natural world objectively in its own terms. He felt nature was our only teacher and that book learning was an important but limited road to the truth. Indeed, he said repeatedly, "Heaven-and-earth is the teacher."[50] We must therefore cast aside all tendencies to project our habitual ways and past knowledge onto the natural world. Indeed, he felt that habits were "enslavements of the mind"[51] that prevented one from seeing the world as it really was. This he considered to be a major obstacle to the discovery of the logic of things, *jori*. He also realized that these habitual perspectives fostered a lack of intellectual curiosity about one's surroundings:

Without feet, heaven turns day and night; without hands, natural creation makes flowers bloom, provides us with children, and brings forth fish and birds. If indeed we are so confined within ourselves, celestial revolutions and natural creations should be objects of great curiosity. Although our curiosity should be aroused about certain things, no one questions them, because we see them before us from morning to evening, passing them by with total unconcern.[52]

One of the continuing habits of human beings was their tendency to anthropomorphize the natural world. Baien wished to break free of this mythical way of perceiving the forces and elements of nature. He felt that humans must not set themselves above or apart from nature and then project their ways onto nature's movements. He wrote:

Man must again put his own interests aside and enter into the world of objects; only in that way can his intellect hope to comprehend heaven and earth and understand all things. All beings exist together with us and we are just one of them. Realization that heaven is universal while man is individual must be the starting point for all discussion of humanity.[53]

This, too, is the new perspective needed for the discovery of nature's logical structure: "There is no systematic truth or logic except that which enables man to comprehend the universe without setting up standards conceived in terms of humanity and human motives."[54]

Thus, Baien combined a religious reverence for the creative processes of nature with a perspective that stressed objectivity in empirical investigation. To know the will of heaven and to assist the transformation of things remain significant spiritual motives behind his observational studies. Yet he struggled to demonstrate that humans need to understand both their connection to the cosmos while appreciating the workings of the natural world on its own terms. An intimacy and a distance, an identity and a differentiation, was needed for authentic empirical studies. Humans ought to understand the larger context in which they undertake such studies while not losing the objectivity necessary for accurate research. In formulating this, Baien repossessed and expanded two central concepts in the Neo-Confucian tradition, namely, the appreciation of the fecundity of the natural world along with an understanding of the principle or order that lies within things.

Jori as Empirical Method and Patterned Structure

Baien enlarged the concepts of principle and the investigation of things to include both an empirical method and a patterned structure. He saw *jori* as a logic of investigation and a logic of form. In other words, it is a dialectical process that has an epistemological aspect and an ontological one. As an epistemological method, Baien urged people first to move beyond habitual ways of thinking and anthropomorphic projections to combine inquisitive doubt with wonder. This was the beginning of empirical investigation. He prompted people to combine doubt with wonder in studying ordinary matters and to begin asking questions at fundamental levels. He suggested, for example, "wondering whether a dead tree might flower, we should find out why it is that a living tree should flower."[55] He further noted that we should inquire into things like thunder, earthquakes, and gravity, which we usually accept unquestioningly.

He advocated careful scrutiny of everything, both in nature and within ourselves. He called for an examination of our sensory powers and our ways of knowing. As an epistemological method of inquiry, then, Baien described the three essential aspects of *jori:*

1. It is essentially dialectical in structure, positing a thesis, an antithesis, and a synthesis.
2. It calls for eliminating all bias and prejudice.
3. It demands empirical verification.[56]

Through this method of inquiry and investigation he felt we would begin to discover the external and internal structure of things.

As an ontological structure, *jori* is essentially "botanical in conception,"[57] with *lo* referring to the branch and *ri* referring to principle or to the grain in wood. As Wm. Theodore de Bary points out, *jori* was a means of describing the external harmony of the natural world and its inner ordering quality.[58] Just as the branches of a tree reflect an external pattern, so does the grain of wood describe its internal structure. While the branches continue to grow and develop, so do the inner rings of the tree reflect a patterned counterpart of that growth. Thus, there is an essential identity between external diversity and inner unity.

Baien's logic, then, is one that is designed to reveal the patterned and textured quality of reality. He saw this as evident in the fact that all living things have an ordered harmonious structure through which the life force passes. For example, human beings have veins that carry *ch'i* and blood through the body. So also do plants and trees have veins that carry energy and water through them. The human likewise creates structures in the natural world based on this concept (e.g., ditches and channels to irrigate fields). He said: "*Li* or patterns [principle] exist everywhere: in heaven and earth, in mountains and in water, in birds and beasts, in fish and turtles, in insects and worms, and even in fungi where the shape is formed by the energy conveyed by its *li* or pattern."[59] *Jori* is the inner ordering pattern that gives shape and form to all reality. To investigate this patterned logic of the natural world was one of the primary tasks of empirical studies for Baien.

Baien noted that using *jori* in investigating things led to true understanding. The key elements of *jori* are eliminating old habits of thought, discerning correct signs from incorrect ones, and being able to see opposites as one. Moreover, the extension of one's knowledge is not achieved through other people but through the direct experience of nature, as well as through empathy with others. One needs to "adopt the method of sympathy and the method of opposition." Sympathy is to understand other people; opposition is to understand heaven and earth. These are part of a continuum for Baien. He wrote:

> . . . there can be no Way greater than that which puts human beings at peace, and there is no skill superior to that which benefits mankind. In this way, from the person of highest station to the multitudes below,

whatever their differences in rank, everyone learns the power of the liveliness of heaven and values the objects it bestows. If we are dedicated to caring for the manifold of creation, could we disregard the great power of heaven and earth?[60]

He noted further that "Joy and sorrow, songs and tears, all these are the work of dynamic flux. If people are able to appreciate fully the function of dynamic flux, they will control themselves well, and treat others well, and may live long in peace under heaven and destiny."[61]

Baien, then, celebrated the creativity of nature in his drive to understand the processes of the natural world. At the same time, he wished to be objective and thorough in his investigations. Thus, he combined the Confucian inspiration to form one body with all things with the empirical drive of science to understand nature's workings. Baien's genius lay in his effort to embrace both the religious and the rational, the moral and the empirical. His dialectical model is an important contribution to Tokugawa thought, and its significance in the premodern period remains to be fully explored.

Baien's Cosmology

In his treatise on natural philosophy, titled *Genkiron,* Baien outlined a comprehensive and detailed picture of the universe and its workings. Minamoto Ryoen has suggested that Baien is writing from the viewpoint of "independent empirical rationalism,"[62] while Rosemary Mercer describes it as an attitude of "scientific realism."[63] Shimada Kenji, however, notes that, "It is my opinion that his philosophy is not, as is commonly said, to be judged as the prenatal stirrings of the concepts of modern science, rather it should be described as the highest culmination of late Confucian natural philosophy."[64]

The fascination of Baien's thought lies in its attempt to respond to the stirrings in Japan of an interest in Western science both as a cosmology for ordering the universe and as a methodology for studying it. Baien's cosmological views were revised some twenty-three times in the *Genkiron* over the same number of years. In its simplest form, the universe for Baien may be described as being filled with the primal *ch'i* (Jp. *ki*): "The one primal ki fills the universe, the tip of the finest hair does not escape it. Dividing and combining, it generates and destroys without cease. The enfolding heaven is outermost, and the earth rests with it."[65]

Baien said there is no room for void because *ch'i* permeates everything in the universe. Hence it supported life in the air, soil, food, blood, etc. The *ch'i* of heaven and earth refers to image and shape, while the *ch'i* of yin and yang refers to going and coming. Heaven turns endlessly, while earth is held motionless in the center. The *ch'i* of yang is warm and light, while the *ch'i* of yin is cold and dark. Yin and yang are the fundamental opposites that make up the universe. Baien described key opposites in the universe, such as heat and cold, water and fire. Furthermore, Baien noted that all objects have their own *ch'i* and no object can exist without it. He accounted for the movement of the one primal *ch'i* as the "motive power." This generates yin and yang, which in turn give rise to shapes with characteristics of soft and hard, large and small, etc.

Conclusion

A century after Baien's death the Meiji restoration had occurred and the modernization process was well under way. The charged debates between technology and tradition, between Western science and Eastern morality, became central to Japan's entry into the twentieth century.

While scholars such as Ekken and Baien could not have fully anticipated the rapid pace with which Japan entered the technological age, some of the problems they raised remain as pressing now as when they first articulated them. How can humans assist in the transforming and nourishing processes of nature through empirical investigation? How can they maintain an intimacy with and a distance from nature that will foster both reverence and objective research? How can humans educate the next generation in ways that are ethical and empirical, humanistic and scientific?

Ekken's answers to these questions tended to emphasize the ethical, namely, the activation of humaneness in the individual, whereas Baien's answers lay more in the empirical realm, namely, the discovery of principle in all things. Yet neither individual was willing to eliminate the religious or rationalistic impetus behind his studies. It is only in our own times that this gap appears to be widening, with still unforeseen consequences. It is appropriate, then, that we should now be raising the same questions that preoccupied these Tokugawa Neo-Confucians. Their concerns, far from being outdated, are as significant now as they were then. They reach across cultural boundaries to speak to the need for a more holistic integration of the religious and the empirical impulses in our own times.

Notes

1. The "Confucian" tradition here refers to the early texts such as the Five Classics, the *Analects, Mencius, Hsun Tzu,* and others. "Neo-Confucian" refers to the later synthesis by Chu Hsi (1130–1200) and others from the tenth to the twentieth century.

2. See Chapter 2 in Frederick Mote, *Intellectual Foundations of China* (New York: Alfred Knopf, 1971).

3. See A. C. Graham, *Disputers of the Tao* (La Salle, Ill.: Open Court, 1989).

4. Process thought is especially indebted to the work of Alfred North Whitehead. See his *Process and Reality* (New York: The Free Press, 1929).

5. See Joseph Needham, *Science in Traditional China: A Comparative Perspective* (Cambridge: Harvard University Press, 1981) and his multivolume series on *Science and Civilization in China*.

6. See the excellent historical survey on science in Japan: Masayoshi Sugimoto and David Swain, *Science and Culture in Traditional Japan* (Rutland, Vt.: Charles Tuttle Co., 1989).

7. See Ronald Dore, *Education in Tokugawa Japan* (Berkeley: University of California Press, 1965); Richard Rubinger, *Private Academics of Tokugawa Japan* (Princeton, N. J.: Princeton University Press, 1982); and Tetsuo Najita, *Visions of Tokugawa Japan: The Kaitokudo Merchant Academy of Osaka* (Chicago: University of Chicago Press, 1987).

8. I will try to speak broadly to both of these points in this chapter, realizing that many other questions still need to be addressed.

9. See the essays in Wm. Theodore de Bary and Irene Bloom (eds.), *Principle and Practicality* (New York: Columbia University Press, 1979).

10. This section on Kaibara Ekken is largely derived from my book *Moral and Spiritual Cultivation in Japanese Neo-Confucianism* (Albany: State University of New York Press, 1989). Another larger version of this section on Ekken appears in *Philosophy East and West* (Jan. 1999), Vol. 48, pp. 5–45.

11. Okada Takehiko, "Practical Learning in the Chu Hsi School: Yamazaki Ansai and Kaibara Ekken," in Wm. Theodore de Bary and Irene Bloom (eds.), *Principle and Practicality* (New York: Columbia University Press, 1979), p. 290.

12. ibid., p. 288.

13. ibid., p. 290.

14. ibid., p. 267.

15. ibid., p. 268.

16. ibid., p. 272.

17. ibid., p. 270.

18. ibid.

19. ibid.

20. ibid., p. 276.

21. ibid., p. 279.

22. ibid., p. 277.

23. ibid.

24. R. Tsunoda et al., *Sources of Japanese Traditions* (New York: Columbia University Press, 1958), p. 367.

25. ibid.

26. Okada Takehiko, "Practical Learning," pp. 283–84.

27. R. C. Armstrong, *Light from the East: Studies in Japanese Confucianism* (New York: Gordon Press, 1974), p. 92.

28. Okada Takehiko, "Practical Learning," p. 259.

29. Kaibara Ekken, *The Way of Contentment* (London: John Murray, 1913), p. 29. Ekken attributes this statement to Ganshi'sui.
30. ibid., p. 61.
31. Miura Baien, "An Answer to Taka Bokkyo," trans. Gino K. Piovesana, *Monumenta Nipponica* 20: 3–4, 1965, p. 442.
32. ibid.
33. R. Tsunoda et al., *Sources,* p. 483.
34. It would seem that, as was often the custom, he divorced his first wives for being childless.
35. R. Tsunoda et al., *Sources,* p. 480.
36. Gino Piovesana, "Miura Baien: 1723–1789," *Monumenta Nipponica* 20: 3–4, 1965, p. 393.
37. ibid., p. 394.
38. ibid., pp. 395–96.
39. Willard Peterson, *Bitter Gourd: Fang I-chih and the Impetus for Intellectual Change.* (New Haven: Yale University Press, 1979).
40. R. Tsunoda et al., *Sources,* p. 480.
41. Miura Baien, "An Answer to Taka Bokkyo," p. 443.
42. *Deep Words: Miura Baien's System of Natural Philosophy,* trans. Rosemary Mercer (Leiden: E. J. Brill, 1991), p. 5.
43. ibid., p. 423.
44. ibid.
45. ibid., p. 440.
46. ibid., p. 442.
47. ibid., p. 397.
48. ibid., p. 400.
49. R. Tsunoda et al., *Sources,* p. 490.
50. *Deep Words,* p. 158.
51. Miura Baien, "An Answer to Taka Bokkyo," p. 422.
52. *Deep Words,* p. 152.
53. R. Tsunoda et al., *Sources,* p. 497.
54. ibid., pp. 487–88.
55. *Deep Words,* p. 155.
56. ibid., p. 427. Also in R. Tsunoda et al., *Sources,* p. 482.
57. ibid., p. 483.
58. ibid. Note that principle is romanized as *li* (Chinese) and *ri* (Japanese).
59. Miura Baien, "An Answer to Taka Bokkyo," p. 428.
60. *Deep Words,* p. 188.
61. ibid., p. 189.
62. de Bary and Bloom (eds.), *Principle and Practicality,* p. 451.
63. *Deep Words,* p. 18.
64. ibid., p. 196.
65. ibid., p. 19.

6 | COSMIC DIRECTIONALITY AND THE WISDOM OF SCIENCE

BRIAN SWIMME

Introduction

In exploring ideas concerning any possible "directionality" to the universe, I shall focus here on the role of the human. I am interested first of all in what can be said from the standpoint of the sciences about any "directions" in which the universe might be moving; and, second, I am concerned with what this scientific understanding might have to say about the basic decisions facing us with respect to our human programs and activities.

In traditional societies there is of course a direct relationship between human actions and cosmic values. But throughout the modern period such a notion made no sense. On the metaphor of the machine, the universe could not be understood as a reality possessing values that humans might incorporate as their own. Thus it was inevitable that all considerations of human goodness would take place without relation to any question of the universe's own dynamics.

Two things have taken place, however, to change our historical situation. First, we have discovered the full range of evolutionary developments occurring over fifteen billion years of cosmological, geological, and biological time. At the very least we now realize that the universe is a developing community of beings, not a machine. And the human community is now understood as being embedded within this evolutionary process. But not only have we developed the technological sensitivities that enable us to observe the changes through cosmological and biological time, we have also developed an ever-deepening understanding of the dynamics of the universe, and this has led to the second major development of the twentieth century: the acquisition of physical knowledge and its use in technological inventions, which has irreversibly altered the nature of evolutionary dynamics.

My main contention, then, is that where previously we could proceed along our evolutionary lines as one species among many, now, armed with our new scientific knowledge and technological power, we are changing the very nature and structure of the whole system out of which we have emerged. And so, our self-understanding must now appropriate this fact. We are individual humans certainly, but we also partake of a wider cosmological and biological dynamic. And understanding ourselves as participating in this more expansive reality, we can ask again, from a very different starting point than before, the fundamental questions concerning the role of the human with respect to the nature of the universe itself.

My aim here is not to attempt to reproduce the sense of coherence between the human world and the cosmos that characterized many traditional cosmologies. I am not sure such a vision of the world is available to us today. On the other hand, I do think that our understanding of directionality in evolutionary dynamics can shed light upon some of the difficult decisions we face in our time. If so, we can consider such light as part of the wisdom that science has to offer humanity here at the start of a new millennium.

Directionality in the Universe

During the twentieth century we have broadened and deepened our understanding of evolution, so that if Darwin could speak of the role natural selection played in creating the great diversity of life around us, we can speak as well of genetic mutation, the formation of the galaxies, the nucleosynthesis in the stars, and the autocatalytic chemical reactions on the planets—all of the intricate interaction within a universe that itself had a beginning and has been expanding for some fifteen billion years. If Darwin was the first biologist to penetrate the surface appearance of things and capture the deep evolutionary nature of life, we have, over the last century and a half, continued this process of discovery so that we not only have empirical data concerning the cosmological, geological, and biological dimensions of evolution, but also a coherent conceptual understanding of the dynamics governing this entire evolutionary process.

Consequently, when we consider the question of cosmic or evolutionary directionality, we do so from a perspective rich in both data and conceptualization of nature's evolution. But even with all of this, we have not been able to arrive at any clear, simple formulation concerning the possible directionality of the evolutionary process. Indeed, precisely because of the complexity of our knowledge, any simple formulation can now be subjected to detailed testing. It was just this more careful examination that led to our rejection of earlier narrowly teleological formulations.

A central question in all this concerns the nature of "spontaneous orderings"[1] in the physical world. We are confronted with the fact of a universe endowed with the potential to construct order. Previous conceptions of a world with an infinity of time, one in which any sort of order could eventually emerge, have now been surpassed with our discovery of a universe that has constructed an immense amount of order in a time frame that is, of course, infinitesimal compared with the chasm of infinity. Thus, it is natural that we now find ourselves once again considering the question of cosmic directionality.

For physicists one of the central questions for contemporary research concerns the formations of galaxies. The universe transformed itself from gas clouds to billions of galaxies all in what amounts to a cosmological instant. That the spectrum of galaxies displays a directional character in the universe is not itself in doubt, only a detailed understanding of the mechanisms by which these constructions were carried out. Similarly, given a cloud of hydrogen and helium in a spiral galaxy with the perturbation of a given nature, we know that stars will result. And given a stellar system with a particular size and mass, we know a supernova will result. Indeed, and most remarkably, physicists now know that given the nature of the four fundamental interactions and given the nature of the initial conditions of the universe, it is fairly certain that the universe would evolve over billions of years to produce galaxies, stars, nebulas, novas, planetary systems, complex minerals, and organic molecules.

To ask whether the conditions at the beginning were shaped by an intelligence or were instead simply the result of random or accidental activity is to divert attention from the truly significant historical development of which we should take note here. Where once scientists regarded questions concerning the directionality of the universe as belonging to the realms of philosophy or poetry or religion, we now explore such questions scientifically with full confidence that we will in time learn more about the nature of the processes of order-production responsible for all of the constructions we find throughout the universe.

Similarly, physical chemists and biochemists[2] examine the complexities of autocatalytic interactions with a growing conviction that the movement from molten matter to early life forms was not an accidental or random happening, but was rather a directional development which, if not inevitable, was at least entirely natural, and possibly even highly probable upon this planet or others like it.

At the present stage of our understanding it is, of course, impossible to say precisely which constructions were truly inevitable, which were highly likely, which were rare, and which were truly unlikely. Physicists would claim that the construction of oxygen was inevitable, while biologists might argue that the particular construction of the eye of the octopus involved innumerable fortuitous events and must be considered extremely unlikely. Given the level of our knowledge of the physical and biological worlds, we are simply nowhere close to being able to assign a probability measure to any particular class of constructions. The point I wish to make here, however, is that given our understanding of fifteen billion years of cosmic evolution, including four billion years of biological evolution, we have begun to see the whole process as a *seamless enterprise* where particles become atoms that become galaxies with stars and planets and complexifying organisms. Some of this constructive activity was inevitable, other constructions were likely, others were probable, still others were highly unlikely, but all of these orderings result from the natural processes of a universe with multiple directions of evolution. It is these directions that I am principally interested in, and that I shall now describe in a general way.

When we think of all that the universe has constructed in fifteen billion years, including the gnat and the shark's brain, it may seem imperious to speak of ever comprehending the directionality of this creative enterprise. It may even turn out to be a dead end. Nevertheless, there are reasons for hope. Consider, for instance, the astonishing diversity that has been constructed with fewer than a hundred chemical elements. Who could have anticipated such an outcome? It is also essential to note that the complexity of life is knit together with a genetic language consisting of only four letters. In addition, all of the known proteins of the living world come from a few dozen amino acids. This is not proof by any means, but it does provide a glimmer of hope that our attempts to articulate the fundamental directionality of cosmic evolutionary process are not necessarily doomed from the beginning.

My assumption here is that the directionality of evolution stems from the interactions of *multiple* processes, none of which are in themselves anything other than the fundamental physical, chemical, or biological processes that natural science has thus far discovered. Nor am I assuming here that there are yet undiscovered forces still operating. Rather, it is precisely the complex interaction effects of the mundane processes studied by scientists worldwide that generate such complex order. Through their interactions, and following highly efficient algorithms, the most ordinary routines have brought forth the enormous variety of order that, as we can now see, has been unfolding for fifteen billion years.[3] Any cosmic directionality, then, would from the point of view of science be the causal outcome of very well understood physical activities in the universe. A star forms out of a cloud of hydrogen and helium because of the gravitational attraction created by the mass of the atoms; a primal animal forms out of unicellular organisms because of the chemical relationships worked out by the cells. The directions in which the universe moves are not something imposed upon the universe but rather arise out of the actions of entities in the universe.

The Cosmogenetic Principle

With these remarks serving as a background I can now formulate what I have elsewhere referred to as the "Cosmogenetic Principle."[4] In an ideal sense, we would like to be able to list the precise directions in which evolutionary dynamics move, no matter what time or place in the universe we are considering. The Cosmogenetic Principle then, as an ideal, would be a description of how matter and energy change through evolutionary processes. Even though the ideal still escapes us, some very keen minds, as we shall see below, have examined the cosmological, geological, and biological data and have given a first articulation to the cosmic sweep of time. Throughout the four-dimensional universe, they tell us, evolutionary process will develop along at least these three lines: expansive differentiation, autopoiesis, and interrelatedness. The basic assertion is that if we observe the universe over time we will find that the evolutionary process brings forth centers of activity that are differentiated, self-organizing, and interrelated.

Furthermore, the basic arrow of time is given by a comparison of space-like slices of the four-dimensional universe as a whole. If one slice consists of systems that are more differentiated (on average), more highly autopoietic, and more interrelated, this slice comes later and is defined to be "more complex."

I need to emphasize that these ideas are based on an examination of the cosmic and biological record rather than any particular theory of evolutionary process. The articulation of these features comes from reflection on the evolutionary data and attempts to surmise various tendencies in the record. The Cosmogenetic Principle is not a theory but simply a summary of these surmises. Even less than a summary, it is a summary of summaries. But for all of its generality it is based upon observation and is in principle falsifiable. To undertake such falsification, one would only need to identify a significant region of the early universe that, over its fifteen-billion-year journey into the present, became ever less differentiated, with subsystems of ever reduced spontaneity, and parts that are increasingly less related to each other.

One might object that this is too vague to be of any use for the question at issue in this book. But the hope is that it represents an early and crude attempt to articulate something quite real about the directionality of the universe. Undoubtedly, if there is any merit in such an enterprise, future scholars will improve upon our current understanding in tremendous and unknowable ways. Since we are indeed the first generation really to see cosmic and biological and cultural evolution during a fifteen-billion-year process as a single, multileveled enterprise, our understanding is necessarily going to be crude.

I will now elaborate on the possible significance of the three tendencies underlying what I call the Cosmogenetic Principle. I shall do so by referring briefly to some of the physicists and biologists who have reflected on the question of a possible directionality to the universe.

Let us look first at expansive differentiation. This is the one characteristic that G. G. Simpson considered to have been pervasive in all organic evolution, manifested in the way life diversifies so as to fill up every available biological opening.[5] Karl Ernst von Baer as well held that differentiation was the fundamental feature of biotic processes. The central direction of all biological change consisted in the way the "homogeneous, coarsely structured, general and potential develops into the heterogeneous, finely built, special and determined."[6] Baer, an embryologist, was thinking primarily of the development of a single organism. But when we think in terms of populations we also arrive at Simpson's conclusion that the number of species increases through time.

This overall movement, though first recognized by reflecting on the biological record, can now be seen to characterize the history of the universe as a whole. We see the expansive differentiation process in the movement from the homogeneous plasma at the beginning of time that broke apart into atoms and then differentiated still further into galaxies and stellar systems. The molten lava of the early Earth that differentiates into oceans and bacteria and further into millions of plants and animals and fungi provides the clearest evidence of expansive differentiation as a general directional tendency over the great sweep of geological time.

Our second feature, autopoiesis (literally "self-creation") or self-organization points to the movement of systems toward relative autonomy. In physical systems this is seen in the movement from the randomness of a gas cloud into the self-organizing activities of a star. In biological systems, it is manifest in the movement that transforms the molecules of the atmosphere and lithosphere into the molecules of the cyanobacteria. Ernst Mayr, considering notions of progress in evolution, refers to a similar idea when he lists "independence of the environment" as a possible measure of progress.[7] Similarly, E. O. Wilson speaks of "control of the environment."[8] In a more detailed way, Francisco Ayala indicates how such independence and control comes about through "the ability to obtain and process information about the environment,"[9] enabling an entity to achieve a certain degree of relative independence. These notions are subsumed by the single concept of autopoiesis, the process of drawing from the environment whatever is necessary for a relatively independent existence. This directional trend leads to an increasing ability of phenomena to adjust to many different environments and includes the development of perceptual capacities.

The third characteristic, that of interrelatedness, points both within, to an organism's internal processes, and outward to its environment. E. O. Wilson refers to this direction as "social organization," while Jeffrey Wicken refers to "functional integration" as a basic tendency of the evolutionary process.[10] More generally, this feature points to the relationships established through natural selection's adaptations that lead to greater efficiency and specialization.

However complex it might be, the history of the universe shows this direction, once again, in the overall sweep of its movement, when the relationships of atoms in clouds are further developed into the relationships of atoms in stellar systems and then in living organs within organisms within an ecosystemic web of connections.

The Terminal Cenozoic

However crude and incomplete, the formulation of the Cosmogenetic Principle is nevertheless truly significant, for it indicates the way in which the human species has not only found its place in space and time, but has even begun the task of understanding the nature of the processes at work in the evolutionary process. If there is any truth in the gropings of the scientists summarized here, we need to stop and reflect on the magnitude of what it means: a single species has developed the power to see into the very center of cosmic and biological evolution.

In order to approach the question of cosmic directionality and what it might imply for human ethical responsibility, we need to discuss a second great discovery of twentieth-century science. The first is the one we have just considered, namely the dynamics of fifteen billion years of cosmic and biological evolution. The second is the discovery that we live in what may be called the *terminal* Cenozoic Era.[11]

Even in classical times, some especially sensitive Greek minds expressed anxiety over the rapid cutting of the forests around Athens with the accompanying loss of topsoil. But humans are adaptable, and in time these anxieties were replaced by a romantic appreciation of the rocky hills of Greece. This pattern appeared again when Europeans first came to the North American continent. Concern about the loss of wilderness resulting from cutting down the continental forests was replaced by admiration for the Yankee ingenuity that was cultivating previously "unproductive" lands. Throughout all the centuries of civilization, almost no one looked at things from the perspective of the Earth's living systems, so that by the time we arrived at the twentieth century the destruction had reached the proportions of a raging fire. In the last fifty years, humans have degraded an area of the Earth larger than all of India and China combined. With such vast habitat destruction comes a loss of species only matched by the mass extinctions. Certainly the extinction taking place in our times is the most extensive in the Earth's systems during the last sixty-five million years.

This information, sobering as it is, is not really in doubt, and can be considered the central message science has to offer the world today. In a document issued by the Union of Concerned Scientists and signed by over 1,600 prestigious scientists,[12] the estimate is given that over the next century the loss of species will be on the order of one-third of all those now living. Certainly species go extinct naturally, but the *rate* of extinction in our time has been pushed up by human activity one hundred thousand times. If the dinosaurs did indeed come to their demise by the impact of an asteroid, then civilized humanity's effect on the Cenozoic Era is on the order of magnitude of an asteroid hitting the Earth.

The Evolution of Evolution Dynamics

If we ask how all of this biological destruction became humanity's principal activity, we are met with a surprise. Humanity has become so destructive precisely because we have continued to move forward in the general direction of evolutionary process. We have become ruinous for the rest of the Earth's organisms because of our very success in moving along the directional lines of cosmic evolution.

Just to comment on this briefly, we can see clearly that in terms of expansive differentiation we have been singularly successful. From a single bag of tools of the earliest humans, we have, over a mere hundred thousand years, developed into huge cities each with over a million different forms of specialized work within an enormously refined technological infrastructure. We have differentiated into every biome, growing from a million or so humans to six billion now and at least ten billion next century.

In terms of autopoiesis, especially when understood as the ability to gather and store and process information about the environment, we have proceeded from markings on deer antlers for the purpose of tracking the moon, to the establishment of the world's libraries and research centers with their microchips and computer data processing. We have been transported so far along the direction of self-organization that we now control the movement and numbers of almost all the megafauna of the planet's continents.

In terms of interrelatedness and social organization, we have moved from the hunting and gathering band with its simple structure involving a single headman to the vast bureaucracies and legislative processes and social groupings of the modern nation state. This social power, combined with the technological power and the sheer numbers of an expanding human species, has led to our current world, where we find ourselves bringing about the end of an entire biological, geological era. So it is not an asteroid that ends the Cenozoic; instead it is a spectacularly successful human species.

We see in this reversal one of the central difficulties in speaking of any such thing as "progress" in evolution. For if we have excelled in extending the three kinds of directionality inherent in the evolutionary process, and if we have actualized so much of the order that is "aimed at" by the evolutionary process, why then—now at the end of the Cenozoic—have we caused such destruction for the entire evolutionary process itself? Should not the furthering of evolution's own tendencies be our mission? Is it not a "good" to become more differentiated, more controlling of the environment, more socially organized?

I will propose for consideration the idea that in order to understand this paradox of a success that is simultaneously a disaster, we need to consider the universe as a whole and over the entire fifteen billion years of its existence. From this wide perspective we can see that the very dynamics of the universe have themselves evolved, in that they have gone through phase changes where the very context of evolution itself has changed. I would suggest that there have been at least three such transitional occurrences. The first is the moment about three hundred thousand years after the cosmic birth when the universe changed from being radiation-dominated to a state of being matter-dominated. In this transitional moment what is significant is not that any of the fundamental interactions themselves changed; rather it is that the *context* for these interactions changed. For instance, if we were to examine the nature of the evolution taking place in the universe when it was only a year old we would need to consider, primarily, the thermal radiation bathing everything. During this epoch, photons determined the very context of, and therefore the possibilities open to, every cosmic event. But after a million and certainly after a billion years things changed in a very basic way, for now the photons were no longer primary. The photons no longer determined the context of evolution, for the matter systems had by now become dominant; and thus from then on the matter systems became the context in which evolutionary dynamics could work.

The second moment to note in this regard is that of the emergence of life. As before, we have here a situation where life, when it first appears, is negligible. In the course of time, however, it expands and eventually becomes an equal partner with the other spheres of the Earth—the hydrosphere, the lithosphere, and the atmosphere. Thus in the early Earth, to understand the evolution of its continents and its mountains and its oceans, one needs to consider only the interactions of matter and energy. With respect to the great constructions taking place, life and its stored information is negligible, just as in the early universe matter was negligible. But after a billion years or so, life's existence proceeds along the very directions of the Cosmogenetic Principle until it arrives at a position of influence. Therefore, to understand the ice ages or the chemical composition of the atmosphere or even the climates, one needs to take into account the presence of life. The context of evolution itself has switched from matter-energy interchanges to one involving matter-energy-information.

Just as the universe moved from radiation-domination to matter-domination, and just as Earth moved from matter-energy interactions to matter-energy-information interactions, so too in our time the dynamics of evolution have again changed in their very nature with the appearance of the human. Two and a half million years ago our presence was negligible in terms of evolutionary dynamics. We were but one species among many. Our effects on the surrounding communities of life were hardly noticed. But now things have changed. After accruing much controlling power during the past two million years, we ourselves are now constructing the very context in which evolution takes place. To take a single example as an illustration we can consider the carbon cycle. The intricacies of the carbon cycle of the prehuman Earth—worked out by systemic interactions over hundreds of millions of years—process two billion tons of carbon through animals, plants, the atmosphere, hydrosphere, and lithosphere each year. But in 1997 humans all by themselves contributed six billion tons to this system. Thus one species alone has now become an equal partner to the atmosphere, the hydrosphere, and the biosphere. In this way and in others, humans are creating a radically new context in which evolution takes place.

We can now see, therefore, that there is a direct relationship between two principal discoveries of the twentieth century. *We humans are the cause of the termination of the Cenozoic precisely because we have gained an understanding of how to control the dynamics of the evolving universe itself.* Furthermore, this very understanding reveals the essence of how the evolutionary dynamics are themselves changing. Stated simply, where for fifteen billion years evolutionary dynamics proceeded in a largely unconscious manner, now, with the human, these same dynamics are unfolding within conscious self-awareness. Stars evolved for billions of years with no human consciousness involved. And yet, now these same fusion processes are understood and activated by human consciousness and expertise. Genetic mutations proceeded for four billion years outside of human consciousness. But now alterations in the gene are being carried out within the human project. For billions of years natural selection organized the evolutionary processes of Earth. But now this unconscious natural selection is being supplanted by a conscious selection: a vast number of species now evolve under pressures created by conscious human decisions.

So we have come to yet another major branch point in the evolution of life and the universe. The context in which evolutionary dynamics will work in the future is permanently changed by the presence of conscious self-awareness. The system of life itself, through the human, reflects upon the entire process of evolution, and in its deepening self-comprehension begins to articulate the directions inherent to the process as a whole.

Granting that human consciousness and human activities have created the basic world in which evolution now takes place, the fundamental question is not, "Is there any directionality to evolution?" but rather, "What possible directions can evolution (through the human) now pursue?" The fate of millions of species will be determined by the answer given to that question. We live in the epochal period in which the future course of evolutionary dynamics are being laid out. Because of the significance of this moment for cosmic evolution, it is not a time for science or scientists to shrink from the challenge posed by such a critical situation. However incomplete our understanding of evolutionary dynamics might still be, it can nevertheless provide us with a basic guidance that takes into account the way in which the universe works in its most basic dimensions.

The Role of the Human

The contribution of science here—what could perhaps be called the wisdom of science—is that of enabling us humans to reflect on our situation from within the perspective of cosmological, geological, and biological evolution. From this context the human is not primarily symbol-maker, nor rational animal nor economic man: The human, in a primary sense, is the space in which evolutionary dynamics operate in conscious self-awareness.

What are the consequences of this new worldview, one that differs from both the traditional and the modernist perspectives? When we conceive of ourselves within evolutionary dynamics, we see that we humans are being offered a larger role, one that is of terrestrial and even cosmic proportions. We are offered the role of enabling the evolutionary process to mutate into yet another modality, that of proceeding within conscious self-awareness. To enter such a larger conception of the human project means that our focus should no longer be on our own species alone. For our decisions are not simply human decisions; our decisions determine the nature of evolution throughout this planet. At the very least we must come to recognize that the norms of reality and value peculiar to smaller contexts such as any particular nation-state or any particular culture, or any particular corporation, are out of proportion to the magnitude of the decisions before us. Our primary concern must be the whole community that will be affected by our decisions, that is the whole community of Earth's life.

The directions of evolution on our planet are today largely determined by the agenda of a tiny segment of the human species. And perhaps this will not change. Perhaps the massive destruction following upon this agenda will continue. But from the data and understanding that 400 years of scientific study has assembled, we can offer another perspective that the human community might consider. We can suggest that the human species, as that space in which evolutionary dynamics now unfurls, could transform or deepen or complete the directions of the evolutionary process in the following ways.

First, in terms of expansive differentiation. Unconscious evolution brought forth an Earth that was never so rich in diversity as when humans first entered into its life two and a half million years ago. We have of course diminished this diversity, but if we were to abandon our exclusive focus on our own expansive differentiation and focus instead on the differentiation of the whole community of life, we would see that for Earth again to achieve such diversity would mean that humans must restrict and over time reduce their numbers. In addition, our technological differentiations must be made with an appreciation of the communities of life in which we reside. This would require difficult changes of many kinds, but the overall guiding principle is easily stated: humans must invent those forms of life and technology that would be mutually enhancing for the life systems of the planet as a whole.

Second, in terms of autopoiesis. This evolutionary tilting toward ever-more efficient mechanisms for obtaining and processing information eventuated, in our own case, in the quality we call consciousness. What is the direction of evolution with respect to the consciousness of a species that understands its larger role in evolutionary dynamics? To the degree that we can alter or influence this consciousness, we need to take seriously the ideal of developing a deeply felt concern for all the components of the Earth Community. Far back in the past, it really did not matter to the processes of organic evolution what humans thought or felt. Consciousness was truly an epiphenomenon with respect to the macrophase evolution of the living systems. But today, and increasingly in the future, the qualities of human consciousness are central to the structure and functioning of evolutionary process. To state the situation in bald fashion: in the past, human thoughts and feelings had nothing whatsoever to do with the emergence of the seals or the pelicans or the forests; but in the future, unless human consciousness is imbued with a profound respect for, concern for, and appreciation of the elephants and seals and pelicans and forests, there are liable to be none of these for all future ages of the Earth.

Third, in terms of interrelatedness. From the perspective of evolution as a whole, there is only one social organization, that of the Earth Society. For human social organization to advance in a way that enables the overall complexity of the Earth Community to advance requires that we take as our goal the challenge of entering into the larger encompassing society. To think of the human society as the ultimate society perhaps made sense in former eras. But within an evolutionary perspective it is without meaning. Now we understand that we are a subsystem of a vaster system and are dependent upon this system for our existence. Our aim must be to join the larger community.

In particular, we need to reinvent human economy so that it operates effectively within the Earth Economy. So long as our human economy is destroying the Earth we are only working against this direction of relatedness, and in ways that will eventually ruin our human economy. In a similar way, we need to reinvent much of human organization so that we can become better adapted to the social relations that have been established throughout the Earth Society over previous hundreds of millions of years. We have become a withering presence for the rest of life. By deepening our efforts in the direction of relatedness we could become an enhancing presence.

This vision of human activity would require a great struggle along with much sacrifice and long periods of time to accomplish fully. But if humans were to enter upon this path, they would not be working alone or in isolation, but would be focusing their efforts along the directions inherent in the needs and desires of every being in the Earth Community.

With all our knowledge and understanding and technological power we should be able to accomplish this. One can even begin to imagine that, should we do so, our decisions would over time lead to a more beautiful and biologically rich planet, a world that is healthy and attractive, and one that we would be happy to hand over to future generations.

Notes

1. I. S. Goerner, *Chaos and the Evolving Ecological Universe* (Langhorne: Gordon and Breach Publishers, 1994), p. 5.
2. Christian de Duve, *Vital Dust: Life as a Cosmic Imperative* (New York: Harper-Collins, 1995), p. 9. See also Manfred Eigen, *Steps Toward Life: A Perspective on Evolution* (Oxford: Oxford University Press, 1992).
3. Brian Swimme and Thomas Berry, *The Universe Story* (San Francisco: Harper-SanFrancisco, 1992), pp. 66–78.
4. ibid.
5. G. G. Simpson, *The Major Features of Evolution* (New York: Columbia University Press, 1953), p. 243.
6. Quoted in Stephen Jay Gould, *Ontogeny and Phylogeny* (Cambridge: Harvard University Press, 1977), p. 61.
7. Ernst Mayr, *The Growth of Biological Thought* (Cambridge: Harvard University Press, 1982), p. 533.
8. E. O. Wilson, *The Diversity of Life* (Cambridge: Harvard University Press, 1992), p. 187.
9. Francisco J. Ayala, "Can 'Progress' Be Defined as a Biological Concept?" In *Evolutionary Progress,* ed. Matthew H. Nitecki (Chicago: University of Chicago Press, 1989), p. 89.
10. Jeffrey S. Wicken, *Evolution, Thermodynamics, and Information* (New York: Oxford University Press, 1987), p. 8.
11. Peter Ward, *The End of Evolution* (New York: Bantam Books, 1994), p. xviii.
12. "*World Scientists' Warning to Humanity*" (Cambridge: UCS Publications, 1993), p. 3.

7 | INFORMATION AND COSMIC PURPOSE

JOHN F. HAUGHT

Most of the issues in science and religion today eventually flow into the largest and most fundamental question of all, that of cosmic purpose. Is it any longer intellectually plausible for us— in this age of science—to think of the cosmos as the embodiment of an all-encompassing meaning?[1] Hasn't the advance of science made it increasingly difficult for educated believers to hold onto the fundamental teaching of religions that *the universe is here for a reason?* The essays by Andrei Linde and Francisco Ayala in this volume have shown how easy it is for scientists and scientific speculation to dispense with considerations of final cause or cosmic purpose. It is not part of scientific method as such to decide the question of teleology. Does this mean, though, that science has thereby left no intellectual room at all for the religious conviction that the universe exists within the embrace of a principle of care capable of redeeming the cosmic process from sheer aimlessness?[2]

Religions have always taught that the cosmos is permeated by a principle of order or meaning. In the Hebrew Scriptures, for example, the universe is the expression of a divine "Wisdom," and in Christianity the cosmos is said to be created in Christ, the eternal *Logos*. Islam views nature as a reflection of the infinite intelligence and compassion of God. Eastern religious thought connects the universe to a principle of "rightness," to *rta, dharma,* or the *Tao,* whereas for Confucians the cosmos has a "moral" character. The universe, in all of these traditional teachings, is much more than just blind and meaningless commotion. The cosmos of religions, as Seyyed Hossein Nasr has indicated in his contribution, is almost universally taken to be the sacramental expression of a transcendent meaning.

Generally speaking, according to classic religious traditions, however, in order to have a meaning or purpose the universe must be structured in a hierarchical way. Religious cosmologies, Nasr points out, embed the temporal world within an eternal and sacred reality immune to transience and death. This means that the lower levels of the cosmic hierarchy are constituted and informed by an ultimate level of meaning flowing down from the highest to the lowest level in a "Great Chain of Being." In fact, the term "hierarchy" originally implied nothing other than that all things have their origin or principle (*arche*) in the domain of the sacred (*hiero*).[3]

However, to many in our own time, modern science has rendered the classical hierarchical vision untenable. In doing so it has apparently made it much more difficult than before for us to think seriously of nature as the sacramental manifestation of an eternal meaning. To the neo-Darwinian scientist, even the functional teleology of organisms, as Ayala claims, has its "ultimate explanation" not in God but in the blind and mechanistic process of natural selection. Thus modern science has seemingly flattened the ancient hierarchical representations of being that for thousands of years made it possible for people all over the Earth to discern a transcendent purpose in the cosmos.

Two closely related developments in the modern scientific picture of nature have conspired to topple the ancient hierarchies in which teleological conceptions of the cosmos originally found their home. We may call these respectively the "atomizing" and the "historicizing" of nature. Today, in spite of growing awareness of the hierarchical and emergent structure of nature, the conviction is still deeply entrenched that life and mind can be made intelligible simply by specifying their subordinate "atomic" components. At the same time, the evolutionary picture of nature portrays life and mind as emerging "horizontally" and gradually—that is, historically—out of lifeless matter lying in the past. Atomism dissolves hierarchies by blurring the crisp boundaries—or ontological discontinuities—that formerly set one level decisively above or below another. And astrophysics has apparently historicized the whole of the cosmos, giving us a picture of nature which, when joined to evolutionary accounts of life, summarily crumples what had been formerly thought of as a vertical hierarchy of distinct levels of being and meaning. In this collapsed, one-dimensional format, nature can no longer easily present itself as the embodiment or expression of any conceivable higher significance.

Atomism—understanding things solely in terms of their fundamental physical constituents—renders the notion of a hierarchical cosmos both illusory and irrelevant. Even though scientists today acknowledge that the physical domain is, in a manner of speaking, hierarchically structured, the kind of "hierarchy" they have in mind is trivial and incidental in comparison with the traditional religious sense of the sharply defined, ontologically discontinuous levels reaching upward toward an Absolute Being. Scientists are aware today that many physical systems nest subsystems, but this kind of hierarchical structuring is relatively inconsequential, since the higher natural systems are generally portrayed as "emerging" derivatively from lower ones without the agency of any supervening principles working from above, and certainly without any divine guidance. The atomistic ideal of explanation assumes that nature in all its wondrous beauty is merely—to cite the British physical chemist Peter Atkins—"simplicity masquerading as complexity."[4] The "ultimate" explanation for the existence and character of what used to be thought of as hierarchically disparate levels of being, each manifesting a sacred meaning in its own way, lies in the irreducible and elemental subordinate physical levels of nature.

A no less momentous challenge to the religious sense of hierarchy—and consequently to cosmic meaning—comes from science's relatively recent discovery that life and mind have emerged rather late in a long historical-horizontal process known today as "evolution." Evolutionary biologists are content to say that living and thinking beings have emerged gradually, and without any directing agency, from an utterly lifeless and mindless material simplicity. Consequently, if the "higher" levels in the older hierarchies have in fact appeared only lately in the meandering and seemingly meaningless chronology of cosmic unfolding, they themselves must now seem, at least to the scientifically informed, as mere derivatives of dumb matter rather than as "higher" and ontologically prior domains of being.

Any notion that the levels of life and mind could have emerged step by step from insensate material stuff without the complicity of a higher principle of being would have seemed completely beyond the realm of intellectual plausibility to the advocates of traditional hierarchical and teleological cosmologies. Such "emergence" would have egregiously violated the principle of causation according to which no effect can ever be greater than its cause. In traditional metaphysics, causation was pictured as flowing downward from the highest level, that of the divine, to the lowest levels. But such an appeal to "higher" causes seemed intuitively much more tenable before we learned, beginning in the last century, how much *time* the evolving universe has actually had available to it in order to concoct living and thinking beings in a purely accidental and directionless fashion.

Accordingly, much scientific thinking now dismisses religious hierarchy entirely. Lacking our contemporary awareness of the vast epochs of natural history that permit a gradual and accidental emergence of life and mind by trial and error, our religious ancestors can perhaps be forgiven for appealing to the notion of a divine cause. Without our new scientific sense of the immensity of cosmic duration, a purely spontaneous and undirected arrival of life would understandably have seemed quite unlikely. Prior to Darwin and Big Bang cosmology, a reasonable search for the explanation of life would apparently have required our positing the miraculous intercession of a supernatural creative agency or vital principle. However, given the immensity of cosmic time uncovered by contemporary cosmology, scientific skeptics can easily suppose that the emergence of life is not so improbable after all, especially if nature was generous enough to provide billions of years for inorganic matter accidentally to become alive and for life eventually—again by a series of random adaptive variations—to become conscious. And if we multiply universes, as some cosmological speculation does today,[5] maybe we can plausibly maintain that the eventual emergence of life has had an infinite amount of time, in which case its improbability is even further diminished. In contemporary scientific thought, it seems, time itself has become so unimaginably ample that its very vastness seems itself enough to transform dead "matter" into living and thinking beings—without any need to invoke the miraculous, or to appeal to hierarchical religious cosmology.

Consequently, time's very magnitude has placed in question the ancient religious habit of positing a hierarchical and meaningful cosmos as the context of life and human existence. Science's temporal elongation of nature's unfolding story now apparently allows time itself to be understood as a causal factor in nature's construction of life and mind, a creative project that we had naively thought of as sustained and animated by God from above. Among evolutionary thinkers today there is a tacit assumption that without immeasurable spans of cosmic time, life's creativity would certainly have been stunted, but that given the actual enormity of nature's duration, blind and random experimentation can build a biosphere without any tinkering from above. As the philosopher Daniel Dennett has recently said, there is no need for "skyhooks" to explain what can be constructed mechanistically over the course of time with "cranes" lifting only from below.[6] "Skyhooks" may have made sense as long as we were ignorant of deep time and the generous latitude it affords for trial and error experimentation. But the discovery of time's unfathomable depths has now dismantled the venerable hierarchical cosmologies in whose ambience previous generations of humans found so much spiritual warmth and redemptive meaning.

At least this is how it looks to many scientific thinkers today. There is apparently no longer any explanatory power in the traditional hierarchical vision, with its assigning higher levels of being a special kind of value, and its endowing the entire cosmos with eternal significance. Modern scientific thought no longer looks to a Platonic realm up above, but only to the lifeless chronological past, for the originating font of those things we value most. In doing so it has broken the spine of what used to be thought of as an integral, vertical constellation of being, meaning, and value. In bringing down the ancient hierarchy it has also, at least for many, shattered the cultural, ethical, and religious structures around which human life on this planet had been organized for thousands of years.

The Task of Religious Thought

It seems, then, that religious thought in this age of evolutionary science and cosmology must face as honestly as it can the question of whether the hierarchical vision that formed the backbone of our great spiritual and metaphysical traditions is in any logically coherent sense recoverable today. Can our theologies, without slipping into absurd contradictions or denying the clear results of natural science, still maintain that the universe is a sacramental expression of an Absolute Source of values, and that it has its origin in the realm of the sacred? Do we any longer have a solid basis for claiming that some things are more valuable than others, and that the cosmos is purposefully influenced by an eternal meaning?

Such an assignment is formidable, as is revealed by the number of ways in which it has been either evaded or deemed impossible by contemporary religious thinkers. It is not necessary for us here to review the well-known renunciations of Darwinian science by Christian fundamentalists. We might note in passing, however, that their negative reaction to evolution is motivated not merely by naive literalism in their interpretation of the ancient religious texts. They also fear that evolutionary science, if it is indeed accurately and adequately descriptive of how life and culture came about, would wreck the precious hierarchy of being and value that lies at the foundation of their entire understanding of reality.

For that matter, even some of our most highly respected religious scholars, those who have no stake at all in scriptural literalism, also often have enormous difficulty mapping the hierarchical metaphysical framework required by their religious faith onto the atomistic and horizontal gradualism of contemporary scientific pictures of nature. Some religious thinkers, of course, have evaded this seemingly impossible project by busying themselves with purely human concerns, putting out of sight the disturbing scientific information about cosmic, biological, and cultural evolution. Their obsoletely dualistic theologies seek to render innocuous the overwhelming scientific evidence that life and humanity have indeed emerged "horizontally" in a very gradual manner over the course of millions of years of adaptive evolution.

How then can contemporary religious thought embrace the horizontal picture of an evolving universe that comes from natural science, without at the same time compromising religion's essential commitment to the ontological primacy of life, mind, spirit, and God? Before offering a response to this challenging task, let us listen first to a religious thinker who has been unusually sensitive to modern science's horizontalizing of the sacred hierarchy that formerly gave meaning and value to life, humans, and the cosmos. Seyyed Hossein Nasr has consistently argued—as he does once again in these pages—that only a hierarchical vision of reality can allow us to locate both nature and humanity within a meaningful cosmos securely rooted in the sacred. Nature can have genuine order and religious meaning only if it is so structured that it can express sacramentally the reality of its divine source. Nasr is keenly aware that modern science, especially Darwinian theory, has for many completely destroyed the ancient sense of hierarchy that for centuries patterned the intellectual and spiritual lives of people everywhere on earth. As a result of scientific modernity's relocation of the origin of things from the sacred "Above" (or "Center") to the profane evolutionary past, many scientifically educated people find it extremely difficult to think of nature as the visible representation of an eternal and absolute reality.

According to Nasr, the consequences of this desacralizing of nature have proved disastrous, no more so than in our thoughtless modern and contemporary destruction of the earth's life systems. The ancient vertical hierarchy of being accorded to life an especially sacred standing, but the horizontalizing and atomizing of nature deprives us of any secure basis for distinguishing clearly between life and the lifeless. Because we have adapted our intellectual life so fully to science's dismantling of the ancient hierarchical sensitivities, we no longer have any good reasons to respect life unconditionally. The significance of the current ecological crisis, therefore, is that it compels us to ponder more carefully than ever the tragic implications of scientific modernity's dismissal of hierarchy.

Nasr thinks that the only alternative to modernity's catastrophic desacralizing of nature is to return to the "perennial philosophy." This is a designation given to core metaphysical beliefs held in common by many native peoples along with the more recent historically dominant religious and philosophical traditions. Foremost among the tenets of the "perennial philosophy" is a belief in an ultimate source of being and meaning, manifesting itself in different ways in each tradition. Nasr writes:

> The traditional interpretation of the *philosophia perennis* sees a single Divine Reality as the origin of all the millennial religions that have governed human life over the ages and have created the traditional civilizations with their sacred laws, social institutions, arts, and sciences. This Divine Reality is beyond all conceptualization and all that can be said of It. . . . Even Its Name remains veiled and unutterable in certain traditions such as Judaism, but Its Reality is the origin of all that is sacred and the source of the teachings of each authentic faith. Like a mighty spring gushing forth atop a mountain, It gives rise to cascades of water that descend with ever-greater dispersion from each side, each cascade symbolizing all the grades of reality and the levels of cosmic and, by transposition, metacosmic reality of a particular religious universe. Yet all the cascades issue from a single Spring and the substance of all is ultimately nothing but that water which flows from the Spring at the mountaintop, the Reality which is the alpha of all sacred worlds and also the omega to which all that is in their embrace returns.[7]

The modern academic approach to religion, as one might anticipate, is quite unsympathetic to the idea of a "perennial philosophy." The hypothesis of a primordial monotheistic origin of the world religions appears especially inconsistent with evolutionary thinking. To most religious scholars, working as they do in a post-Darwinian academic atmosphere, the perennial philosophy is the product of an intellectual abstraction that ignores the actual historical and developmental stages in the rise of human culture and religious traditions. Nasr would probably reply to them, however, that the academic study of religion has already been warped by the historicizing horizontalism that evolutionary thinking has noxiously introduced into the academy. And because academic religious studies have already embraced a temporal-historical rather than a metaphysical appreciation of religion, they are impotent to place us in touch with the divine.

Along with its insistence not only on the metaphysical, but also the historical, primacy of an absolute and ineffable Sacred Reality, the perennial philosophy also insists upon the irreducibility of the higher to the lower levels in the hierarchy of being. Thus it appears to conflict with the methodological agenda of modern science, which seeks to explain the things we value most in terms of lower-level lifeless and mindless entities and processes that seem, both to religious sensibility and common sense, to have considerably less importance and less reality than life itself. What we need instead of *modern* science, according to Nasr, therefore, is a *sacred* science, one that opens human awareness up to the full range of levels of being in the cosmos. Here he joins with other devotees of the perennial philosophy, e.g., Fritjof Schuon, Huston Smith, and E. F. Schumacher, who would also argue that the hierarchical vision has to be upheld lest all the beliefs of traditional religion and cultured and ethical human existence come tumbling down.

Nasr has hereby raised an issue that religious thinkers who embrace evolutionary science and molecular biology's reductive method need to face more explicitly: Is it logically possible to embrace simultaneously the religious-hierarchical and the modern scientific viewpoints? Can we accept the evolutionary understanding of life and mind as emerging out of "matter," without at least implicitly surrendering our traditional sense of their "sacred" origin?

Nasr's erudite writings stubbornly refuse to allow the evolutionary paradigm to bring down the timeless and indispensable sense of hierarchy without which all values and meanings would dissolve. Some version of hierarchy, he rightly insists, is essential to any satisfactory conception of cosmic meaning as well as to the adequate grounding of ethical and legal precepts. Essential, it seems, to any doctrine that life and mind have a sacred origin, or that our moral norms are more than just human conveniences, is a way of thinking about the world in which subordinate levels (or dimensions) can be quietly informed by "higher" levels (or deeper dimensions) that are more comprehensive, more real and more valuable. Hierarchical ordering is absolutely essential if some things are to have more value and meaning than others and if human life is to avoid being reduced to chaos. We need not picture hierarchy in a rigidly vertical manner—we can think, for example, of circles embedded within wider circles—but to deny the hierarchical principle altogether would render impossible the attribution of enduring importance to anything at all. It would discourage any of our efforts to formulate a substantive ethic. And here we must agree with Nasr, it would also undermine our attempts to forestall the modern desecration of the natural world.

Religious Hierarchy and the Idea of Information

I shall now argue, however, that a religiously hierarchical vision can, after all, form a plausible alliance with the scientific atomizing and historical-horizontal understandings of the universe that have apparently leveled the cosmic hierarchy of traditional religions. It is quite possible, I believe, to wed the hierarchical vision of being and value on the one hand with the new molecular, evolutionary, historical, and horizontal picture of life on the other. Thus we can make ample room for both science and religion in our contemporary understanding of the universe.

We may begin the task of forging such an alliance by noting once again that hierarchical thinking is not completely absent even within the world of science. Today the most stalwart scientific reductionists acknowledge that "lower" levels of physical reality are nested within "higher" ones. Today there is a rapidly expanding awareness that science cannot cleanly account for "higher levels" of complexity solely by analysis of the "lower." What gets lost if we try to explain a higher level only in terms of the atomic particulars of a lower level are the "informational" arrangements that give complex beings their distinctive reality. By "information" I mean here simply the organizational sequencing of subordinate elements as well as the "patterning" that gives things their identities.

Today science is increasingly, though sometimes grudgingly, acknowledging that information is an inherent aspect of nature. "Information" is a metaphor used by scientists to express the inevitably somewhat vague intuition that there is more to nature than just combinations of matter or transformations of energy in time. There is also an elusive ingredient that gives pattern, order, or form to things and processes. Information does not stand out as something that science can hold onto, for it is non-massive and non-energetic. Still, it effectively organizes or patterns natural objects or processes so that things can fall naturally into hierarchically distinct domains.

Even though it does not exist separately from actual concrete beings, the informational aspect of nature is still logically and ontologically distinguishable from the natural continuum of atomic constituents and the historical sequence of causes involved in nature's evolution. Because of this "timeless" and independent character of information, hierarchical discontinuity can emerge in the cosmos simultaneously with, and alongside of, what scientific method envisages as an unbroken continuum of material and historical causes. From its purely "objectifying" point of view, all that science can make out in nature may be atomic units or historically tight causal chains of events. But there is plenty of room left alongside all of this for informational discontinuity, and hence hierarchical structuring, within the natural continuum. It is a serious logical mistake to deny the informational discontinuity in nature's hierarchy simply because it does not manifest itself by dramatically interrupting the atomic and historical continuity featured by modern scientific portraits of nature. Discontinuous levels of information can easily be inscribed within what appears to the methods of chemistry, physics, or evolutionary science as sheer material and historical continuity. It is the residence in nature of different levels of informational ordering that now allows religious thought legitimately to affirm the enduring validity of hierarchical thinking. The idea of information allows us to map the hierarchical onto the horizontal after all. Nature, then, can be thought of as structured hierarchically even while it appears to science as an unbroken atomic or historical plenum.

In its surprising encounter with the informational aspect of nature, science itself has now come up abruptly against a kind of causation radically different from what it had been accustomed to dealing with. Of course, the notion of *formal* cause has an ancient pedigree, both in philosophy and theology, but along with explanation by final cause it was dropped as unimportant in modern science. Science until recently has been concerned almost exclusively with efficient and material causes. It has had little interest in taking into account a kind of causation that works morphologically, non-materially and non-energetically. Scientists today, however, are beginning to acknowledge more explicitly the role of information and patterning, especially in the phenomena known as chaos and complexity.

The most obvious example of informational and, consequently, hierarchical ordering in nature, however, is that associated with DNA. In DNA's molecular structure it is the informational sequence of four acid bases—A, T, C, and G—that quietly bestows on each living organism a distinctive identity. As Michael Polanyi has convincingly argued, the specific informational sequence in a DNA molecule is logically irreducible to the chemical processes operative in the living cell.[8] Chemistry does, of course, helpfully describe the properties of the atoms and molecules essential for life, but these properties do not by themselves determine the particular ordering of nucleotides in any given instance of life. Since almost any arrangement is in principle chemically possible, the informational sequence in the DNA molecule that makes a living organism become an amoeba, a cockroach, a frog, or a human person is distinguishable from the invariant laws of chemistry and physics in which the information is embodied.

The question arises then as to just how information does its work. How can something so quiet and concealed as information be so effective? Aristotle and Plato would have found such a question peculiar, since both of them gave prominent causal status, though in very distinct ways, to "form" in their attempts to understand the natural world. Modern science, though, looks for the efficient and material causes of things, and so it has usually suppressed questions about how things get their actual identities. Yet at least in some of the most recent science, nature's puzzling tendency to organize itself "spontaneously" has brought renewed attention to the role of form and information in the constitution of complex adaptive systems. "Information," taken here in a very broad sense, is the designation we may give to whatever it is that integrates atomic constituents (atoms, molecules, cells, genes) into comprehensive wholes. Science cannot specify the comprehensive function of informational patterning by gazing either at the atomized particulars or at the historical-horizontal process out of which they have emerged. Information operates comprehensively and so, by definition, cannot itself be comprehended in terms of the particulars it integrates into concrete wholes.

But, once again, how does this mysterious thing called "information" really function if it is so intangible? Since we cannot answer this question in conventional scientific terms, perhaps we can find some illumination in the world's religions. Here the ancient Chinese body of religious and philosophical wisdom known as Taoism may offer some guidance. The *Tao Te Ching,* a text attributed to Lao-Tzu (sixth century BCE) refers to the Tao, the ultimate, unnameable Way or Truth in which the world is grounded, as like water, or a valley, or an uncarved block. All of these share the trait of being able to bring about momentous results while themselves remaining unobtrusive and energetically inactive. It is this kind of self-concealing power which, according to Taoism, shapes the whole of the cosmos. We may think of the role of information in nature along similar lines. The Tao is not itself part of an objectively identifiable set of things or events in the world. It remains materially unobtrusive and energetically passive. Nevertheless we may say, at least analogously, that it is informationally active. Indeed, its very absence from the matter-energy continuum is what allows the Tao to exercise its comprehensive influence on the world. If the Tao were itself part of the physical or temporal continuum, and therefore easily available to our objectifying consciousness, it would be powerless to integrate components into identifiable wholes. The Tao is effective only because of its humble, self-withdrawing character known in Taoism as *wu wei,* an untranslatable term for "active inaction" or "non-interfering effectiveness." Perhaps information "works" in a similarly hidden and humble manner.

Physical science, for its part, can observe only things that are prominent, empirically available, and energetically forceful. Taoism, however, points to the real potency residing in a "Way" that does not stick out in any such manifest way. The Tao that shapes nature is so devoid of prominence that one cannot even give an appropriate name to it. It recedes behind, beneath, or beyond all phenomena. It is not to be found among the things that impress our senses. Yet it is all-powerful in its self-withdrawal:

Thirty spokes are joined at the hub.
From their non-being arises the function of the wheel.
Lumps of clay are shaped into a vessel.
From their non-being arises the functions of the vessel.
Doors and windows are constructed together to make a chamber.
From their non-being arises the functions of the chamber.
Therefore, as individual beings, these things are useful materials.
Constructed together in their non-being, they give rise to function.[9]

The philosopher Wu Cheng (1249–1333) comments on these images: "If it were not for the empty space of the hub to turn round the wheel, there would be no movement of the cart on the ground. If it were not for the hollow space of the vessel to contain things, there would be no space for storage. If it were not for the vacuity of the room between the windows and doors for lights coming in and going out, there would be no place to live."[10]

Is it conceivable that information—again taken in its most generic sense—makes itself felt at the levels of matter, life, mind, and the universe as a whole in this non-interfering manner of influence? If there is universal purpose to cosmic process, Taoism instructs us that we would be sensitive to it only after we ourselves have learned the wisdom of *wu wei* and allowed our lives to be reformed accordingly. Scientific investigation, focusing—figuratively speaking—on the spokes, the clay, the window, and door frames, rather than on the "nonbeing" that forms and shapes their very identities, must itself fall silent when it arrives at the threshold of the void that allows specific things to be themselves and become functionally active. Awareness of the non-interfering effectiveness of information, or of the quiet presence of cosmic meaning, could occur to us only after we have ourselves undergone a personal transformation in which the Taoist humility and sensitivity to the power of non-being has begun to reshape the center of our own lives.

In Christianity, especially as articulated in the theology of St. Paul, there has been a parallel conviction that God's power can be made most transparent in weakness and humiliation, (1 Cor 1:17–31). An intuition of what we may justifiably call "the humility of God" is perhaps one of the most important insights humans have ever had about the nature of ultimate reality. But such insight is not reducible to, or verifiable, in terms of scientific understanding. Thus the *Tao Te Ching* says:

Gaze at it; there is nothing to see.
It is called the formless.
Heed it; there is nothing to hear.

It is called the soundless.
Grasp it; there is nothing to hold on to.
It is called the immaterial.
Invisible, it cannot be called by any name.
It returns again to nothingness.[11]

Somehow the effectiveness of ultimate reality with respect to nature is registered not in spite of but rather because of its silent non-availability. The intuition of Taoism as to what is most powerfully influential makes somewhat pretentious the modern philosophical and scientistic demand that everything that is truly real should reveal itself phenomenally. The view that the totality of being should fall within our grasp is, according to these traditions, a most crippling attitude, one ultimately rooted not in a humble desire to know but in the irrational excess of a will to dominate reality. The Taoist approach to knowledge suggests that a genuine sensitivity to the real must look beneath the outward obtrusiveness of things:

Numerous colors make man sightless.
Numerous sounds make man unable to hear.
Numerous tastes make man tasteless.[12]

Beyond ordinary objects and sensations lies the undifferentiated fullness of the Tao.

Contemplate the ultimate void.
Remain truly in quiescence.
All things are together in action,
But I look into their non-action.[13]

There is no straightforward logical argument that will convince us that informational power can be present in the non-action of *wu wei,* just as logical arguments are not enough to convince warmakers that nonviolence can be more effective than force. To embrace the Taoist attitude is fundamentally a matter of conversion, and logical arguments will probably never convey to the proponents of scientism the conviction that divine influence in the world does not have to take the form of *ad hoc* interruptions of the natural world that we can expect to show up empirically.

In Christian terms, likewise, God's capacity to influence the world is not in spite of but rather because of the Creator's humble, self-emptying restraint and refusal to express the divine effectiveness in crass, coercive forms of action.[14] The universe is the product of a divine *kenosis* (emptying). The demand by modern scientism that the fullness of reality should make itself available to our empirical grasp seems exceedingly cheap when held up against the delicacy of religious visions in which real power has the character of humility. That all of reality must subject itself to the human mind's control would appear, when contrasted with these traditions, as the most impoverishing of imperatives.

Therefore, because scientific method is cognitionally inadequate to detect the humble presence of *wu wei* (non-action), or divine *kenosis,* it would understandably be insensitive also to any purposeful hierarchical ordering. However, by acknowledging the role of information in nature, science shows that it is nonetheless, in principle at least, open to the possibility that nature can be arranged into formal hierarchical discontinuities, even though physical continuity of the sort represented by atomistic and historically horizontal portraits of an evolving cosmos is what typically catches the scientific eye.[15]

The presence of informational discontinuity can render the idea of hierarchy plausible, as Nasr's thought demands, without there being any systematically measurable disturbance of the continuum of nature as portrayed by contemporary science. For, as we have just seen with the help of the Taoist point of view, the presence and effectiveness of information simply cannot make itself visible at the level of purely physico-chemical or evolutionary analysis. The informational sequence in DNA, for example, can be dramatically effective—introducing sharp discontinuity into nature—without in any way "intruding" into the molecular or historical continuum of nature evolving.[16]

Let us use a simple analogy to make the point.[17] With a pen trace a meaningless, unbroken marking on a piece of paper. Then, without lifting your pen off of the paper write a word or phrase. While forming the word or phrase you are in no way altering the chemistry of ink and paper that was operative while you were just scribbling. When viewed only from the perspective of the chemistry of ink and paper there is a physical continuity between the unintelligible scribbling on the one hand and the intelligible word or phrase on the other. But viewed from another point of view, that of information, there is obvious discontinuity. The sudden appendage of informational content to your pen's markings does not interrupt the physical continuity when it introduces informational discontinuity. At the level of purely chemical analysis, nothing new is going on when the informational arrangement of letters in an alphabet is suddenly introduced. And from the point of view of an atomizing and historicizing perspective, the absurd scribbling and the intelligible writing form an unbroken continuum. Yet, from an information-sensitive perspective, there is radical discontinuity.

The point of the analogy is simply that atomic and evolutionary continuity in nature do not logically preclude hierarchical discontinuity. An informational sequence can unobtrusively configure an array of nucleotides in DNA without in any way interrupting laws of chemistry, physics, or evolutionary process. Likewise there is no obligation on the part of religion to accept the claim that the natural sciences—even with their atomizing and historicizing tendencies—have in the slightest way logically destroyed the discontinuity proper to religious hierarchy, or the sense of cosmic purpose that requires hierarchical embodiment. At the same time, therefore, there is no logically compelling reason why religious people should not also fully endorse and promote the scientific understanding of nature.

Notes

1. See Steven Weinberg, *The First Three Minutes* (New York: Basic Books, 1977), p. 144, and Alan Lightman and Roberta Brawer, *Origins: The Lives and Worlds of Modern Cosmologists* (Cambridge: Harvard University Press, 1990).
2. For a much expanded version of the ideas presented here see my book, *God After Darwin* (Boulder, Colorado: Westview Press, 2000).
3. See Nasr's chapter in the present volume, pp. 42–57.
4. Peter W. Atkins, *Creation Revisited* (New York: W. H. Freeman, 1992), pp. 11–17.
5. See Andrei Linde's essay in this volume.
6. Daniel C. Dennett, *Darwin's Dangerous Idea: Evolution and the Meaning of Life* (New York: Simon & Schuster, 1995).
7. Seyyed Hossein Nasr, *Religion and the Order of Nature* (New York: Oxford University Press, 1996), p. 12.
8. Michael Polanyi, *Knowing and Being,* ed. Majorie Grene (Chicago: University of Chicago Press, 1969), pp. 225–39.
9. *Tao Te Ching,* trans. Chang Chung-yuan, *Tao: A New Way of Thinking* (New York: Harper & Row, 1975), Chapter 11.
10. Cited by Chung-yuan, p. 36.
11. *Tao Te Ching,* Chapter 20.
12. ibid., Chapter 24.
13. ibid., Chapter 25.
14. Jürgen Moltmann, *God in Creation,* trans. Margaret Kohl (San Francisco: Harper & Row, 1985), p. 88.
15. Michael Polanyi shows that our use of the idea of information imports into science ineradicably personal, tacit, and unformalizable aspects of human knowing. In fact it is only because we are capable of recognizing meaning that the notion of information even shows up at all in our scientific discourse. Take, for example, biologists' use of the notion of information to specify what the DNA molecule is and what it does. Even as materialist and reductionist a

biologist as Richard Dawkins refers to the DNA as a digital "river of information" flowing out of Eden. But it is not the digital units themselves—the nucleotides, ATCG—that are informational. Rather, as Polanyi shows, it is the *specific sequence* of letters that bears the information. And this sequence is extraneous to what chemistry and physics can specify. See Polanyi, *Knowing and Being,* pp. 225–39.

16. See Polanyi, *Knowing and Being,* pp. 225–39; *Personal Knowledge* (New York: Harper Torchbooks, 1964); and *The Tacit Dimension* (Garden City: Doubleday Anchor Books, 1967).

17. This analogy is suggested by Polanyi in *The Tacit Dimension,* pp. 31–34.

8 IS THERE DESIGN AND PURPOSE IN THE UNIVERSE?

OWEN GINGERICH

The southern cliff face of South Plaza Island in the Galápagos is the nesting grounds of the swallow-tailed gull, the world's only night-feeding gull. As the gray-and-white birds flit in and out like swallows, a characteristic mark identifies this unusual gull: a white dot on the bird's black bill. This distinctive feature provides a pecking spot where, in the near darkness, the chicks can peck to signify that they want to be fed. William Paley, the English divine who early in the nineteenth century wrote *Natural Theology; or, Evidences of the Existence and Attributes of the Deity Collected from the Appearances of Nature,* would undoubtedly have seen this as "a mark of contrivance, in proof of design, and of a designing Creator."[1] In contrast, today's evolutionists would rank this as a curious and ingenious, but probably typical, adaptation, something naturally selected over many generations for its survival value.

As the naturalist and paleontologist Stephen Jay Gould says, "Every naturalist has his favorite example of awe-inspiring adaptation."[2] His is the fish-like appendage found in several species of the freshwater mussel *Lampsilis*. Like most clams, *Lampsilis* lives partly buried in bottom sediments. "Riding atop the protruding end is a structure that looks for all the world like a little fish. It has a streamlined body, well-designed side flaps complete with a tail and even an eyespot. And, believe it or not, the flaps undulate with a rhythmic motion that imitates swimming." When a real fish comes by to investigate the phony fish, the clam discharges its larvae; some will be ingested by the fish and find their way to its gills, where they can mature.

The biological world is replete with astonishing examples of intricately interwoven adaptations. Surely our intuitive reaction is to extol the ingenuity and elegance of the design, and to follow Paley in seeing this as the work of a designing Creator. This notion of design suggests, of course, the existence of a goal-directed or end-directed process, which can aptly be termed teleology. But ever since the work of Charles Darwin over a century ago, an alternative, entirely naturalistic scenario has also been on the table. In particular, Darwin drew attention to imperfect adaptations, where nature seems to have worked molding the materials at hand for a new environmental niche, but in which the design sometimes seems less than optimal. Consider the red-footed booby, a duck that nests in the trees on Genovesa Island in the Galápagos. How ridiculous, a duck precariously balancing on a branch, its webbed feet barely providing a grip! No wonder that Ernst Mayr, a leading evolutionist, has written that "cosmic teleology must be rejected by science—I do not think there is a modern scientist left who still believes in it."[3] So much then, for the role of a Creator in modern biological science.

While we can envision the various biological adaptations slowly but naturally emerging over countless generations with selection tediously taking place out of hundreds or thousands of random mutations, it is much more problematic to think of the universe itself accidentally emerging as a fit place for intelligent life. So, despite the articulate denials of cosmic teleology by the leading evolutionists of our age, there still remain enough astonishing details of the natural order to evoke a feeling of awe. In the opening moments of the big bang, and in the patterns of stellar evolution, everything seems astonishingly well tuned for a universe in which self-conscious life can emerge.

This particular argument of cosmic "fine tuning" has been impressively honed in recent years. One way in which the matter-energy density of the universe expresses itself is in the general curvature of space on the grand scale. Astronomers have found that the universe is very close, ambiguously close, to being Euclidean. To use the current idiom, space is nearly flat, even though it may seem an oxymoron to call three-dimensional space "flat." Incredible as it may seem, in the first split second after the big bang, the initial universe must have been extremely flat for the universe to be nearly flat now, because any small deviations would have been immensely magnified in the expansion. The requisite flatness is about 1 part in 10^{59}; this is a stupifyingly large number, one that expresses the incomprehensibly precise balance between the energy of expansion and the gravitational potential energy.[4] Had the original kinetic energy of the big bang explosion been less, the universe would have fallen back onto itself long before there had been enough time to build the elements required for life and to produce from them intelligent, sentient beings. Had the energy been more, the density would have dropped too swiftly for stars and galaxies to form.

To Princeton physicists John Wheeler and the late Robert Dicke, these and many other details were so extraordinarily finely tuned that it seemed the universe had been expressly designed for humankind. Even small variations in some of the constants of nature would have led to a universe in which life could not exist. Such was the original context that led to the anthropic principle, the idea that, like the little bear's porridge, our universe was "just right" as a home for humankind. (This is a principal interpretation of what is often referred to as the strong anthropic principle.)[5]

On this particular issue, however, the past decade has brought about a sea change in astronomical opinion. A sub-scenario, one that does not invalidate the big bang theory, but a theoretical speculation that offers a further new twist, has been added to the history of the first split second of the universe. Called "inflation," it describes an unimaginably swift expansion in the opening stages of the universe. In effect, it brings down a curtain over the earliest moment of creation, blurring out the initial conditions, and flattening the universe with high precision. Instead of saying that the universe started off by incredible chance or by supernatural design to a tuning of 1 part in 10^{59}, skeptics can point to inflation to say that it makes no difference what the initial tuning was, because the exacting flatness has been built into the universe by the inflation mechanism.

However, for those who are awed by the insinuations of design, does it make any difference whether this aspect of the design came about seemingly without cause, or by an even higher level of design in the physics of the universe itself? In any event, the evidence of design is so ubiquitous that scientists who wish to deny its implications have had to cope with its presence, essentially by giving the phenomenon a name: the anthropic principle. Briefly stated, they have turned the original argument on its head. Rather than accepting that we are here because of a deliberate supernatural design, they claim that the universe simply must be this way *because* we are here; had the universe been otherwise, we would not be here to observe ourselves, and that is that. (This is generally called the weak anthropic principle.)[6]

In one of his many splendid essays, the late Jacob Bronowski wrote that the world is divided between those who think of men as machines, and those who refuse to accept the idea of men as machines. "I have a great many friends who are passionately in love with digital computers," he wrote. 'They are really heartbroken at the thought that men are not digital computers."[7] It is plain that Bronowski did not number himself among them. Among my own friends are some who fiercely believe that we are machines and that the universe itself has no discernible purpose. Probably nowhere is this credo so starkly stated as at the end of Steven Weinberg's *The First Three Minutes:* "The more the universe seems comprehensible, the more it also seems pointless."[8] I passionately disagree with these ardent and articulate champions of the gospel of meaninglessness. Yet I cannot prove to them that we are *not* mere machines or that the universe has a purpose any more than they can prove to me that I am an automaton in a meaningless cosmos. In trying to produce logically infallible proofs for the existence of supernatural design in the universe, we reach a standoff.

Purpose and Design

Nevertheless, most of what we accept, in either science or our own understanding of the world, derives not from logical proof, but from a web of belief that I can simply describe as *coherence,* the way things hang together and make sense. And it is within that search for coherence that evidences of design are particularly interesting.

Now the title of my paper, pressed upon me by the organizers of this symposium, has both the words *design* and *purpose.* Design generally implies purpose or intention, but purpose is rather different from design. In an earlier essay I had used the word design somewhat loosely, and I was criticized by the philosopher Mortimer Adler for falling victim to a central error in modern natural theology.[9] He reasoned that if the universe was unfolding according to a preordained blueprint, there would be no place for freedom or free will, and hence the idea of design bordered on heresy. I had intended the word "design" to suggest not a rigid plan, but a framework in which intelligent, rational, self-conscious life could emerge, and that is how I use it here, recognizing that intention or purpose might carry the nuance more accurately.

So let me now review several curious details of the cosmos, without which we would not be here today. I have already mentioned the extraordinarily fine balance between the kinetic energy of the original explosion and the gravitational attraction of the parts that tend to pull the universe back together again. Without this balance we could not have a large and old universe filled with structure. But why do we have such a vast cosmos? Can we find anywhere a starker example of profligate wastefulness? Yet here is a modern paradox: the block the builders rejected has become the cornerstone. Cosmic antiquity now seems a necessity for the ultimate emergence of life, and with age comes size. We now understand the role of billions of years, possible only in a cosmos of vast dimensions. We see the long-drawn-out chemical evolution in the life and death of generations of stars. Slowly there emerges a chemically enriched universe with a small but extremely relevant fraction of heavier elements necessary for the complexity of life—iron for hemoglobin, to name just one.

One of the first scientists to consider how the chemical environment itself made life possible was the Harvard chemist L. J. Henderson. In 1913, well after Darwin had emphasized the fitness of organisms for their various environments, Henderson wrote a fascinating book entitled *The Fitness of the Environment,* which pointed out that the organisms themselves would not exist except for certain properties of matter. For example, he argued for the uniqueness of carbon as the chemical basis of life, and many things we have learned since then, from the nature of the hydrogen bond to the structure of DNA, reinforce his argument. But today we can go still further and probe the origin of carbon itself, all the way to its synthesis in the cores of evolving stars.

Carbon is the fourth most common element in our galaxy, after hydrogen, helium, and oxygen. A carbon nucleus can be made by merging three helium nuclei, but a triple collision is tolerably rare. The process would be easier if two helium nuclei would stick together to form beryllium, which could be the stepping stone to carbon, but beryllium is not very stable. Nevertheless, sometimes, before the two helium nuclei can come unstuck, a third helium nucleus collides with the pair, and a carbon nucleus results. And here the details of the internal energy levels of the carbon nucleus are very intriguing: as it happens, there is precisely the right resonance within the carbon to help this process along.

Let me digress a bit to remind you about "resonance." You have no doubt heard that opera singers such as Enrico Caruso could shatter a wine glass by singing just the right note with enough volume. I don't doubt the story, because in the lectures at our Science Center at Harvard about half a dozen wine glasses are shattered each year using sound waves. It's necessary to tune the audio generator through the frequency spectrum to just the right note where the glass begins to vibrate—the specific resonance for that particular goblet—and then to turn up the volume so that the glass vibrates more and more violently until it explodes with a bang. The resonance in the carbon nucleus is something like that, except that it enables the pieces to stick together rather than fly apart.

In the carbon atom, the resonance just matches the combined energy of the beryllium atom and a colliding helium nucleus. Without this finely tuned resonance, there would be relatively few carbon atoms. Similarly, the internal details of the oxygen nucleus play a critical role. Oxygen can be formed by combining helium and carbon nuclei, but the corresponding resonance level in the oxygen nucleus is half a percent too low for the combination to stay together easily. Had the resonance level in the carbon been four percent lower, there would be essentially no carbon. Had that level in the oxygen been only half a percent higher, virtually all of the carbon would have been converted to oxygen. Without that carbon abundance, neither you nor I would be here now.

I am told that Fred Hoyle, who predicted the existence of this remarkable nuclear arrangement, has said that nothing has shaken his atheism as much as this discovery. I have never had enough nerve to ask Sir Fred if his atheism had really been shaken by finding the nuclear resonance structure of carbon and oxygen. However, the answer came rather clearly in the Cal Tech alumni magazine, where he wrote:

> Would you not say to yourself, "Some supercalculating intellect must have designed the properties of the carbon atom, otherwise the chance of my finding such an atom through the blind forces of nature would be utterly minuscule." Of course you would. . . . A common sense interpretation of the facts suggests that a superintellect has monkeyed with physics, as well as with chemistry and biology, and that there are no blind forces worth speaking about in nature. The numbers one calculates from the facts seem to me so overwhelming as to put this conclusion almost beyond question.[10]

Sir Fred and I disagree about lots of things, but we concur about the presence of design in the universe. And both of us would agree that the carbon-oxygen resonances are only the tip of the design iceberg.

To pursue the evidences of design further, let me turn from the cosmos on the grand scale to the earth itself, and to the curious history of its atmosphere. Everyone who keeps up with the news is aware of the greenhouse effect, a phenomenon ominously linked to the fragile but alarming evidence of global warming. There is probably little need to recite what the greenhouse effect is, but some readers may be surprised to learn that the greenhouse effect is vital for life on earth. The temperature at the top of the earth's atmosphere is about 25°C *below* freezing; down here at the blanketed surface it averages 20°C above freezing. Without the greenhouse effect, the earth would be a frozen globe.

Early in the history of the earth, four to five billion years ago, the sun was significantly dimmer, and water, which was abundant in the primordial material out of which our planet formed, would normally have been frozen solid. This freezing may well have happened repeatedly, only to have the solid oceans thawed out by energetic planetesimal impacts. But eventually a thick atmosphere of carbon dioxide formed, producing enough greenhouse effect to keep the oceans liquid. However, as every consumer of carbonated beverages should appreciate, CO_2 is highly soluble in water. Throughout the ages vast quantities of CO_2 dissolved in the earth's oceans and then precipitated out in the form of limestone, gradually removing enormous amounts of the powerful CO_2 greenhouse gas from the atmosphere.

This scenario stands in marked contrast to our neighboring sister planet Venus, where the temperature was just enough higher to keep the water vapor gaseous, which was therefore unable to dissolve CO_2. As the sun's luminosity slowly increased, a runaway greenhouse effect developed on Venus, guaranteeing hellish surface temperatures and preserving a thick blanket of CO_2, with an atmospheric pressure a thousand times greater than on earth.

Meanwhile, something even more astonishing was happening on earth. A primitive form of photosynthetic life had appeared, over three and a half billion years ago, which began to release free oxygen into the atmosphere. Free oxygen is a deadly poison to primitive organisms but an essential source of energy to more complex ones. Roughly a billion years ago the oxygen level of the air reached ten percent, the critical amount needed for the formation of an ozone layer, something absolutely required to shield off the destructive solar ultraviolet radiation. Without the ozone, the living organisms would have been fried by sunlight. The incredible timing of this process, which reduced the greenhouse effect in synchronism with the increase of solar luminosity, amazes all the astronomers I know. In reviewing this scenario for my Core Science class at Harvard, I could only conclude by saying, "It's a miracle."

Contingency and Life

To the theist *or* the atheist, the scenario of the earth's evolving atmosphere must be something wondrous to behold. Whether such a miracle implies the existence of a superintelligent designer, or a benevolent deity, is another matter. There is clearly no proof here, but then again, science does not work primarily by proof, at least proof in the sense of Euclid or positive logic.

But let me go on. Among the principal planets of our solar system (and I here exclude Pluto), our earth is unique in having such a comparatively large companion as the moon. Chemically the moon is very different from the earth, and therefore the moon had a quite different origin from that of the earth. The most probable scenario seems to be that a Mars-sized (or perhaps somewhat larger) planetesimal impacted the earth in its early stages. Most of the iron from that colliding body sank to the core of the heavily disrupted earth, and the moon coalesced from the stony debris still orbiting our planet. The impact gave the principal spin to the earth, leaving a swift rotational period of several hours. The moon was then much closer to the earth, and consequently there were huge, scouring tides that washed nutrients into the oceans far more effectively than our rivers do today. This contingency must surely have enhanced the pace of biological evolution. Meanwhile, tidal friction has gradually slowed the earth's rotation, and, in accordance with the conservation of angular momentum, the moon has slowly retreated.

From the growth patterns of fossil Devonian corals and Ordovician brachiopods, and from daily tidal deposits in ancient Indiana limestones, it has been possible to determine both the length of the day and of the lunar month in the Paleozoic period. By the late Precambrian, just under a billion years ago, the earth's rotation had slowed to a period of roughly nineteen hours. This was the same time that the oxygen abundance had risen sufficiently to allow for more complex, oxygen-consuming organisms and the invention of sexually reproducing eukaryotic cells with their genetic information stored in cell nuclei. Now the reproductive cycle could jump from a matter of hours in the light of one day to a much longer period of weeks, provided the organisms could cope with intermittent light and darkness. We are now on very technical biological ground far from my own expertise, so let me quote from a paper by a specialist, Professor Gary Rosenberg of Purdue University:

> According to current chronobiological thinking, . . . circadian rhythms in living organisms can be shortened to periods substantially less than 17–19 hours only with difficulty. . . . This has prompted many chronobiologists to believe that there is within all Metazoa [that is, multi-celled creatures] an inherited, internal clock which times physiological processes to a 24-hour period and which is independent of environmental cycles.[11]

In other words, Rosenberg argues that a day of nineteen hours or longer was required for the sort of biochemistry that could keep an organism actively functioning through a nighttime period when photosynthesis was not available. Such a length of day—nineteen hours—was achieved at roughly the same time that the oxygen abundance was right for more complex organisms. This, then, was the threshold of the great Cambrian explosion, "Evolution's Big Bang," as *Time Magazine*'s cover proclaimed a few years ago.[12]

Now if we look more closely at these various examples, we see that they represent several different manifestations or levels of design. The biological adaptations can be seen as William Paley saw them, as evidence of a designing Creator; alternatively, they could be a planless pattern of natural selection. On the other hand, the cosmological theology, the sort of examples used in connection with the anthropic principle, such as the energy balance of the big bang or the carbon-oxygen resonances, are details built into the universe at its very beginning. As we might say, they are part of the original blueprint, and they have characterized the action in the universe for more than half of its existence. On the other hand, the marvelous miracle of the felicitous evolution of the earth's atmosphere seems more connected with the specific happenstance of our solar system, a minute part of the universe as a whole. And, in the case of our planet's rotation, there seems to be even less of design and more of accident.

In citing these provocative ideas, I have moved away from the idea of design, the results of the architect's good planning, to *contingency,* the accidental behavior of history that so impresses many of our most profound evolutionary theorists. Here I cannot expand further on the role of contingency, although I could have mentioned the asteroidal impact 65 million years ago that may have administered the *coup de grâce* to the dinosaurs. It is difficult to convey the shock that the acceptance of such a catastrophic event has produced among uniformitarian geologists. As one distinguished paleontologist has asked concerning the dinosaur extinction, "Bad genes or bad luck?" and it has been hard for evolutionists to concede that bad luck may be the answer.[13]

From our point of view as an emerging human species, this bad luck was crucial, because it gave our miniature primate ancestors space and time to proliferate and evolve. There were further narrow escapes, such as when the rodents nearly took over, but I think I have made my point about the role of contingency, the seemingly accidental, in the story of our strangely nurturing universe.

Contingency and Purpose

To a theistic scientist, and perhaps even to God, a world with contingency is far more interesting than one devoid of it. Seen with the eyes of faith, the world seems to be organized with purpose, direction, a pervasive sense of movement toward higher organization, but not necessarily with a total blueprint. It is a universe of uncertainty and chaos. God may well have *intended* self-conscious, contemplative beings, quite possibly in many different latent possibilities fully known to the Creator, without specifying which of these possibilities would actually be realized. The more we look at the universe, the more it appears to be constructed with an innate freedom, with a fundamental role for contingency. This is a rather awesome thought. It means that maybe it is not in the terrestrial plan for everything to come out all right in the end. It means that we have some freedom to shape the destiny of human civilization, including both the freedom and the power to end it through greed, selfishness, and downright carelessness. This, then, is the implication of contingency.

If the purpose of the universe is for the emergence of intelligent contemplative life, it could well happen many times in the vastness of the universe. Those of us who are theists have no brief to limit God's creativity to a single self-conscious species. There is a long tradition for this stance, going back to the thirteenth century, when in 1277 the Bishop of Paris declared that it was heretical to limit the powers of God as Aristotle had seemingly done when the Greek polymath declared that the basic principles of philosophy denied the idea of a plurality of worlds.[14] Nevertheless, when we look at the incredible configuration of contingency that has brought us to this remarkable home for mankind, we cannot be too confident that it would happen twice. Perhaps, like a giant plant whose sole purpose is to bring forth one small, exquisite flower, our universe is now achieving its purpose.[15] This is an arrogant statement, I know, but at the same time exceedingly humbling because of the burden of responsibility it places on us all. How tragic it would be to nip the flower in its bud! It behooves us to take the greatest of care lest this fragile flower wither too soon.

Summary

Let me now summarize the argument I have outlined. From its opening moments, the universe is singularly and amazingly constructed to allow for the emergence of self-contemplative intelligence, a suitable home for humankind. To the theist, the heavens declare the glory of God, and the firmament exhibits God's handiwork. To the atheist, these marvels are mere facts, neither evidences nor pointers, and surely not proofs of God's intentions or designs.

But even an atheist must concede that our universe has a history, and part of that grand sweep of history includes the emergence of our earth as a habitable and inhabited planet, the specifically suitable home for a humankind endowed with creativity, conscience, and self-consciousness. And when we look in detail at this history, we see the role of contingency, which signals to the theologian that God has deliberately built an element of freedom into creation, which brings the awesome responsibility of choice to us, created in God's own image.

As a scientist, I am fascinated by unifying principles that give us insights into how the universe works and how it has evolved over time. I like both the grand picture and the intricate details of the tapestry we call natural science. I like the way these scientific explanations make sense. As a contemplative human being I am impressed by the creative achievements of humankind, from the paintings at Lascaux to the *Divine Comedy* to the Ten Commandments and theory of relativity. Perhaps the purpose of the universe is simply for contemplative observers to exist in awe of a superintelligent designer; perhaps it is something more. For the universe as a whole to make sense, I hold with those who favor purpose. The search for that ultimate purpose is a serious, essential, and often deeply mysterious, part of our earthly pilgrimage.

In conclusion, we might consider the words of the seventeenth-century virtuoso and author Sir Thomas Browne: "The wisdom of God receives small honour from those vulgar heads that rudely stare about, and with a gross rusticity admire his workes; those highly magnifie him whose judicious enquiry into his acts, and deliberate research into his creatures, returne the duty of a devout and learned admiration."[16]

Notes

1. William Paley, *Natural Theology; or, Evidences of the Existence and Attributes of the Deity Collected from the Appearances of Nature* (Edinburgh: William Whyte, 1816), Chapter 5, section 5, p. 61.

2. Stephen Jay Gould, *Ever Since Darwin* (Norton: New York, 1979), p. 104.

3. Ernst Mayr, "The Ideological Resistance to Darwin's Theory of Natural Selection," *Proceedings of the American Philosophical Society*, 135 (1991), 131.

4. Alan Lightman and Roberta Brawer, "An Introduction to Modern Cosmology," in *Origins: The Lives and Worlds of Modern Cosmologists* (Cambridge: Harvard University Press, 1990), esp. p. 23.

5. See John D. Barrow and Frank J. Tipler, *The Anthropic Cosmological Principle* (Oxford: Oxford University Press, 1986), pp. 21–22.

6. ibid., pp. 16–21.

7. Jacob Bronowski, *The Origins of Knowledge and Imagination* (New Haven: Yale University Press, 1978), p. 109.

8. Steven Weinberg, *The First Three Minutes* (New York: Basic Books, 1977), p. 154.

9. See "Kepler's Anguish and Hawking's Query: Reflections on Natural Theology," and "Response to Mortimer Adler," in M. J. Adler and J. Van Doren (eds.), *Great Ideas Today 1992* (Chicago: Encyclopaedia Britannica, 1992), pp. 271–86 and 302–04. Adler's reply is on pp. 287–301.

10. Fred Hoyle, "The Universe: Past and Present Reflections," *Engineering and Science*, November, 1981, 8–12.

11. Gary D. Rosenberg, "Growth Rhythms, Evolution of the Earth's Interior, and Origin of the Metazoa," *Geophysical Surveys,* 7 (1985), 185–99.
12. *Time Magazine,* cover story, December 4, 1995.
13. David Raup, *Extinction: Bad Genes or Bad Luck?* (New York: Norton, 1991).
14. Steven J. Dick, "Natural Law Versus Divine Omnipotence," in *Plurality of Worlds: The Extraterrestrial Life Debate from Democritus to Kant* (Cambridge: Cambridge University Press, 1982), Chapter 2.
15. I have borrowed this metaphor from physicist John Wheeler.
16. Thomas Browne, *Religio Medici* (London: Andrew Crooke, 1642), p. 28.

INDEX

Adaptation: adaptive radiation, 26; in evolution, 25–28; from natural selection, 32; promoted by natural selection, 24; teleological mechanisms as, 30; teleological mechanisms in organisms as, 30–32
Adler, Mortimer, 124
Albrecht, Andreas, 7
Anthropic principle: discussions in Islamic philosophy of, 54; examples used in connection with, 129; interpretation of, 123; relation to teleology in nature, xv; strong, 123; weak, 123
Aquinas, Thomas, 20
Arabi, Ibn al-, 43
Aristogenesis, 36
Aristotle, 51, 130
Atkins, Peter, 107
Atomism: defined, 106; effect on hierarchies, 106–7
Augustine, 29–30
Autopoiesis: in Cosmogenetic Principle, 96–97, 99; defined, xv, 97
Ayala, Francisco, 97, 106

Baer, Karl Ernst von, 96
Bergson, Henri, 36
Big bang theory: predictions of, 1; questions about standard assump-

tions of, 1–2; rate of expansion of the universe, 5–6
The Bridgewater Treatises, 20
Bronowski, Jacob, 123–24
Browne, Thomas, 131

Causality: in Indian thought, 60; *Sankhya* system, 63
Causation: time as factor in construction of life and mind, 108; in traditional metaphysics, 107
Cenozoic Era, 97–99; humans as cause of demise of, 101
Chaotic inflation, 7–8, 12
Coherence: search in the cosmos for, 124
Confucianism: Chinese, 73–74; Japanese, 79–82; in premodern Japan, 69–73. *See also* Neo-Confucianism
Consciousness: conceptions in Indian thought, 64–66; human understanding of the universe, 101–3; in materialistic doctrine, 15; possible degrees of freedom in, 15; unsolved problem of, 16
Cosmogenesis: Arabic and Persian vocabularies dealing with, 43–44; Islamic Metacosmic Principle in, 48; in Islamic thought, 43–47; question of, 43; Sufi terms for, 44

133

Cosmogenetic Principle: as an ideal, 95; autopoiesis characteristic of, 96–97, 99; expansive differentiation characteristic of, 95–96; interrelatedness characteristic of, 97, 99

Cosmogony: in Indian context, 60

Cosmological principle, 3

Cosmology: of Confucianism, 69–70; explanation of inflationary, 3; meaning of term, 42; of Miura Baien, 87–88; modern cosmologies, 42; source of the universe, 2; theory different from inflationary theory, 6

Cosmology, Islamic: cosmologies, 42–51; God as creator of the world, 44–49

Cosmology, quantum: concept of consciousness in, 14; question of creation of the universe in, 10–13; role of observer in, 14

Cosmos: biblically based notion of, xv; evolution and dissolution in Indian thought, 62–64; evolution as seamless enterprise, 94–95; Indian views of, 63–64; purpose in Indian thought, 59–61, 67; purpose of, 105; religious view of, 105–6; shaped by self-concealing power (Taoism), 115. *See also* Teleology; Universe

Creation: Arabic and Persian meanings of, 43–45; creative process in Confucianism, 69; Sufist terms related to, 44

Darwin, Charles, 122; on adaptive variations, 22; theory of natural selection, 19–24, 27–28, 39

Dawkins, Richard, 41n10

Dennett, Daniel, 108

Dicke, Robert, 123

Diderot, Denis, 40n1

Divine Principle (Islam): hierarchy below, 49–50; necessity of, 46; relation between cosmos and, 43

Earth: importance of greenhouse effect, 126–27; origin of rotation of,

127; ozone layer, 127; photosynthesis on, 127–28

Einstein, Albert, 4, 5

Eternal inflation, 9

Evolution: adaptive combinations in, 25; directional development in, 93–97; explanation of biological, 19; natural selection does not direct, 36–37; position of life and mind in process of, 107–8; role of chance in, 27; role of mutation in, 27; selection process in, 24–25; as teleological process, 33–37; twentieth-century understanding of, 92

Evolution of the universe, 93–94; directionality of, 92–96; process in, 95; transitional occurrences, 99–100

Explanations, causal: compatible with teleological explanations, 37–39

Explanations, teleological: of biological phenomena, 29–30; circumstances for, 28; compatibility with causal explanations, 37–39; purpose and requirements of, 32

Filiality (Ekken), 77–79

Galaxies, 93

Gliner, Erast, 6

God: as creator in Indian thought, 61; as creator of the cosmos (Islam), 43–47; as creator of the world, 4–5; as designer of organisms' adaptation, 20–21

Gould, Stephen J., 121

Guth, Alan, 7

Heliocentrism: in Miura Baien's thought, 81–82; of sixteenth- and seventeenth-century thought, 20

Henderson, L. J., 125

Hierarchy: atomism's effect on, 106–7; linking science with religious, 112–19; in perennial philosophy, 111–12; religious sense of, 106–8

Hoyle, Fred, 126

Human species: control of dynamics of the universe, 101; evolution on earth, 100–101; future role, 101–3; place in space and time, 97–98

Inflation of the universe, 123; chaotic, 7–8, 12; eternal, 9; Guth's model, 7; Linde's theory, 7; Starobinsky's theory, 7
Information: function in contemporary science, xv; function of, 114–15; in hierarchy of science, 113–14; intangibility of, 115
Investigation, empirical: Miura Baien's contribution to, 85–86
Islam: cosmologies of, 43–50; debates about creation of the world, 45–48; Quranic doctrine of universal hierarchy, 49; teleological nature of universe, 52–53; Ultimate Reality of, 48–49; views of nature, time, space, etc, 43. *See also* Divine Principle (Islam)

Kaibara Ekken, 70, 73–79
Kaluza-Klein theory, 15
Karma: pan-Indian concept of law of, 60
Kirzhnits, David, 7

Lamarck, J.-B., 36
Lao-Tzu, 115
Logic: Miura Baien's search for, 683–85

Matter: before theory of relativity, 14
Mayr, Ernst, 97, 122
Metacosmic Principle (Islam), 48
Miura Baien, 70
Monopoles: effect of universe's inflation on, 6–7; as prediction of big bang theory, 1–2
Moon: relation to earth, 127–28
Mutations: available to natural selection, 27
Mythology, Indian, 64

Nagel, E., 37
Nasr, Seyyed Hossein, 106, 110–12

Nature: in ancient Indian context, 61–62; in Confucian cosmology, 69–70; in Ekken's philosophy, 74, 76–79; hierarchical ordering in, 114; Indian attitudes toward, 66–67; informational aspect of, 113–14; in Miura Baien's philosophy, 79–80, 82–85; modern scientific view of, 106; twentieth-century perception of, 92–95; views in premodern Japan, 70–73
Neo-Confucianism: Chu Hsi as synthesizer of, 73–74; of Kaibara Ekken, 73–79; of Miura Baien, 79–88
Nomogenesis, 36

Okada Takehiko, 76
Order: in context of Indian cosmogony, 60; hierarchical order of nature, 114; universe as constructor of spontaneous ordering, 93
Organisms: adaptation of, 18–32; adaptive organization of, 26–28; as internal teleological systems, 35; natural selection designs, 27; teleological explanation for certain, 18–19, 29; teleological mechanisms and structures in, 30–37; teleological properties of, xiii; without teleological explanations, 32–33
Orthogenesis, 36

Paley, William, 20, 121
Particles, electrically charged, 3–4, 7
Perennial philosophy: hierarchical vision in, 111–12; tenets of, 110–11; views of religious scholars about, 111
Polanyi, Michael, 114
Principle: Miura Baien's contribution to concept of, 85–86, 88

Quantum field theory: physical field fluctuations, 8–9

Radiation, adaptive, 26
Relativity theory, 14
Religion: modern academic approach, 111; religious hierarchy, 112–19

Rosenberg, Gary, 128
Rushd, Ibn, 45

Sadr al-Din Shirazi, 45, 47, 51
Sakharov, Andrei, 6
Sankhya system, 63
Scalar fields: quantum fluctuations of universe's, 8–9; relation to inflation of the universe, 7–8; theory of, 3–4; in weak and electromagnetic interaction theory, 10
Schumacher, E. F., 112
Schuon, Fritjof, 112
Science: atomistic explanation, 106–7; changing role of information in, 114; discoveries related to origin and fate of the universe, 10–16; discovery of biological and cosmic evolution, 97–98; discovery of potentially terminal Cenozoic Era, 97–98; effect on religious view of the universe, 106; in Ekken's philosophy, 76–77; explanation of the universe through, 20; hierarchical thinking in, 113; linked to religious hierarchy, 112–19; Nasr's advocacy of sacred, 112; used in exploration of the universe, 93
Science, Western: in modern Japan, 88; in premodern Japan, 69–73; rise of, 72
Selection, natural: central argument, 21–22; conscious selection supplants, 101; as creative process, 18, 22–25; Darwin's theory of, 19–24; factors influencing outcomes of, 36; generation of novelty by, 23–24; genetic mutation and recombination in, 30–32; homeostatic mechanisms from, 31; modern understanding of, 22; as nonrandom process, 24; as opportunistic process, 26; process of, 18, 26–28; as stepwise process, 24–25; as teleological process, 34
Self-regulating systems: from natural selection, 31; teleology of, 29–30
Simpson, G. G., 96
Sina, Ibn, 44–45
Smith, Huston, 112

Space: existing and changing with time, 14–15; quantum fluctuations of physical fields in, 8–10; before theory of relativity, 14
Space-time: compactified dimensions, 4; four-dimensional, 4–5, 16; in general theory of relativity, 14; in Islamic philosophy, 51; of special relativity, 14
Species extinction, 98
Starobinsky, Alexei, 7
Steinhardt, Paul, 7
Structures, functional: teleological explanation for, 30
Super-gravity theory, 15
Superstring theory, 12, 15
Supersymmetric theories, 15

Taoism, 115–17
Tao Te Ching, 115–17
Teilhard de Chardin, P., 36
Teleology: attitude of modern science toward, 57n27; bounded (or necessary), 18, 35; concept of, 19, 28; external (or artificial), 18, 34; of inanimate objects, 31–33; internal (or natural), 18, 34–35; of organisms, 28–31; of self-regulating systems, 29–30; specific and generic levels, 33; unbounded (or contingent), 18, 35. *See also* Explanations, teleological
Time: cosmic time, 108; in current scientific thinking, 108–9; in four-dimensional universe, 95; Islamic investigation of, 50–52; in Islamic philosophy, 47; Islamic quantitative, 51–52; in schools of Indian thought, 62–65; before theory of relativity, 14; in wave function of the universe, 13–14. *See also* Space-time

Uniqueness problem, 4–5
Universe: beginning of expansion of, 2; conception in sixteenth and seventeenth centuries, 20; directionality of evolution of, 91–96; evidence of design of, 123–26; evolution of dynam-

ics of, 99–101; expansion and rate of expansion, 5–8; flatness of, 2; homogeneity of, 3, 6; immortality of, 9; in Indian thought, 62; inflationary domains of, 9–10; inflation of, 6–9, 123; Miura Baien's perception of, 81, 82, 87–88; moral purpose of Confucianism, 69–70; nonhomogeneities in, 6, 8; question of source of original, 2; scalar fields of, 4–5, 7–10; scientific knowledge of, 91–92; self-reproducing inflationary, xii, 9–10; twentieth-century understanding of, 92; uniqueness problem of, 4–5; vacuum structure of inflationary, 8; yin and yang in (Confucianism), 70. *See also* Cosmos; Evolution of the universe; Inflation of the universe; Teleology; Wave function
Utility as criterion, 38–39

Vaisesika system, 62–63
Venus: greenhouse effect on, 127

Wave function of the universe: to describe universe's evolution, 13; time-independence of, 13–14
Weinberg, Eric, 7
Weinberg, Steven, 59–60, 124
Wheeler, John, 123
Wheeler-DeWitt equation, 13
Wicken, Jeffrey, 97
Wilson, E. O., 97
Wu Cheng, 116